RENAISSANCE

Boris von Brauchitsch

BARRON'S

Front cover from top to bottom and left to right:
Luca Signorelli, The Resurrection of the Flesh (detail), Cappella di San Brizio, Cathedral,
Orvieto / Dome of St. Peter, second half of the 16th century, Vatican, Rome / Andrea
Mantegna, *Camera degli Sposi* (detail of ceiling fresco), 1465–1474, Palazzo Ducale,
Mantua / Benozzo Gozzoli, The Procession of the Three Holy Kings (detail), 1459–1461,
Palazzo Medici-Riccardi, Florence / Piero della Francesca, Portrait of Federico da
Montefeltro, ca. 1472, Galleria degli Uffizi, Florence / Rogier van der Weyden, The Depo-
sition from the Cross (detail), ca. 1435, Museo del Prado, Madrid / Benvenuto Cellini,
Perseus, 1545–1554, Loggia dei Lanzi, Florence / Fra Angelico, Mocking of Christ, 1440,
San Marco, Florence / Titian, Reclining Venus, ca. 1538, Galleria degli Uffizi, Florence
Back cover from top to bottom:
Matthias Grünewald, Crucifixion (detail), Isenheimer Altar, 1512–1516, Musée
d'Unterlinden, Colmar / Leon Battista Alberti, facade of Santa Maria Novella, 1456–1478,
Florence / Michelangelo Buonarroti, The Creation of Adam (detail), 1511–1512, Sistine
Chapel, Vatican, Rome
Cover background: Jan Gossaert, Sketch sheet with studies of ancient sculptures,
ca. 1508/09, Rijksuniversiteit, Leiden
Frontispiece: Filippino Lippi, Portrait of a Young Man, ca. 1485, National Gallery of Art,
Washington, Andrew W. Mellon Collection

First edition for the United States and Canada published by
Barron's Educational Series, Inc., 2000.

First published in Germany in 1999 by DuMont Buchverlag GmbH und Co.
Kommanditgesellschaft, Köln, Germany

Text copyright © 1999 DuMont Buchverlag GmbH und Co.
Kommanditgesellschaft, Köln, Germany.

Copyright © 2000 English language translation, Barron's Educational Series, Inc.

English text version by: Agents - Producers - Editors, Overath, Germany
Translated by: Sally Schreiber, Cologne, Germany
Edited by: Bessie Blum, Cambridge, MA

All inquiries should be addressed to:
Barron's Educational Series, Inc.
250 Wireless Boulevard
Hauppauge, New York 11788
http://www.barronseduc.com

International Standard Book No. 0-7641-1336-4

Library of Congress Catalog Card No. 99-65090

Printed in Italy
987654321

Contents

Preface

Presenting a brief overview of the epoch of the Renaissance is an undertaking as challenging as it is subjective, because the number and diversity of Renaissance personalities both mandates selection and makes it difficult. It is impossible to approach historical topics without preconceived notions, and particularly in discussions of the Renaissance, these concepts all too often do not advance beyond pat character studies of princes and artists. Consequently, the myth of the Medicis as "inventors" of the new era is as questionable as the heroic histories of "great men" with protagonists such as Michelangelo, Leonardo and Raphael. Similarly, interpretations of the age which claim a transformation from a martial age of iron into a golden and more peaceful period are not made more convincing by the fact that contemporaries already held these views.

Even in the Renaissance, the rise of a banking family to great political power—for example, the case of the Medicis of Florence—remained the exception. Such an ascent naturally required a new form of homage, since the traditional honor reserved for ancestry and martial prowess were no longer appropriate. The formula "pax et libertas," which Cosimo de' Medici engraved on his coins, in no way implies greater peace and liberty, but instead chiefly reveals a tradition of empty political slogans, with which we still contend today. Nonetheless, the innovations in the arts and sciences during the 15th and 16th centuries are so diverse that the epoch of the Renaissance is justly seen as the beginning of the modern age.

This survey attempts to comprehend the era of the Renaissance as a network of inspirations. To be sure, many individuals contributed extraordinary works to this network, but they cannot be appreciated except as parts of a greater constellation. "It did not require the Renaissance to discover the individual," according to E. H. Gombrich, "and yet, there is a kernel of truth in Giambattista Vico's interpretation of history: Only with the end of the age of heroes could the age of man begin."

It cannot do any harm if historians of the Renaissance occasionally pay heed to this view of the past.

Boris von Brauchitsch

1304–1374
Francesco Petrarch and Giovanni Boccaccio (1313–1375) attempt to revive Latin and Greek studies

1316
Italian anatomist Mondino de Luzi dissects corpses and writes a definitive anatomy text

1341
Petrarch crowned with laurel in Rome as poet laureate according to ancient custom

1347
Cola die Rienzi attempts to re-establish ancient Roman Republic

ca. 1396
Humanists begin to study and translate ancient Greek as well as Latin authors

1400
Fillio Brunillischi: first excavations of ancient Rome

The age of discoveries

The Renaissance has successfully established its own myth. Both the creative spirits of the Renaissance and its later scholars and admirers have proudly defined the Age of Humanism as a new beginning after the barbarism of the Middle Ages. The contrast between the "rising sun" of the Renaissance and the supposedly dim epoch of the medieval world remains a popularly accepted notion today. The innovative spirits of the 15th and 16th centuries understood Humanism both as a philosophical position and as an approach to intellectual enlightenment that included an emphasis on the fine arts. In actual practice, however, the personal and political life of the age was still subject to an arbitrariness that was only vaguely reconcilable with the theoretical ideals of the new epoch.

The earliest harbingers of the coming Humanist separation of religion from research, of faith from knowledge, had already begun to appear during the late Middle Ages. The process moved with increasing speed, but brought deep crises in its train. Scholars such as Copernicus, Kepler, and Galileo typified the desire to ground science on fact, measurement, and perception free from dogma. Such figures embodied the courage of the new scientific investigations that discredited the traditional understanding of the relation of the planets and the sun, thereby allowing a completely new understanding of the world. This daring critical approach went hand in hand with the development of

Martin van Heemskerck, *View from the Capitol onto the Roman Forum*, ca. 1535. Engraving, Kupferstichkabinnett, Berlin.
Heemskerck was in Rome from 1532 to 1535 and wandered daily through the city, sketching ancient and contemporary works. No one reproduced the antique treasures so faithfully as Heemskerck.

The Myth of an Epoch

The French term *Renaissance* was derived from the Italian word *Rinascimento*, meaning in general a rebirth of a past era, and in particular the revival of Roman antiquity in the late 14th century, the era between the Gothic and the Baroque, that marks the beginning of modernity. As a designation of a period in art history, the term first came into use in the early 19th century. The idea of a rebirth of antiquity, however, was already prevalent during the Renaissance itself. Indeed, Giorgio Vasari spoke of *rinascimento* in many of his *Lives*, but meant to convey rather an attitude of spirit than any particular artistic style or a term for an epoch. He understood the age in which he lived as the continuation of a brilliant imperial epoch, of which one possessed only literary knowledge. The sculptor Lorenzo Ghiberti, in his *Comentarii* (written ca. 1450), quoted extensively from the ancient authors Pliny and Vitruvius, and pointedly described the disintegration of the Middle Ages and the "revival" of art after 1300.

Traditionally, art historians have divided the epoch into an Early Renaissance (around 1300–1500), a High Renaissance (around 1500–1530), and a Late Renaissance, also known as the age of Mannerism (around 1530–1600).

revolutionary new techniques and tools for investigating the world and disseminating knowledge. This was the age that invented the telescope and the printing press, rediscovered and reinterpreted the legacy of the ancient classical world, and prepared the foundations of modern science.

But it was also the age of the Inquisition—an integral component of the ecclesiatical system from the early Middle Ages until (officially) the Second Vatican Council in 1965. When the Inquisition began to gain influence in Italy in the wake of the Counter-Reformation, the ultimate irreconcilability between free inquiry and Platonic teachings, on the one hand, and Christian doctrine, on the other, became dramatically evident.

Individual and despot

In its glittering display of elemental contradictions, the Renaissance shines forth as one of the most brilliant periods of history—and therein lies the source of its fascination for generations of historians. It almost seems that every aspect of the age has already been completely described, catalogued, analyzed and comprehended. After all, new texts surprise the world only at greater and greater intervals, and the restoration of artworks is a one-time event, bringing only slight

1416
Poggio Bracciolini discovers complete manuscript of *Instituto oratoria* by Roman rhetorician Quintilian (d. 95 A.D.) in a monastery in St. Gallen, Switzerland; great influence on the development of Humanism

1428
Italian Humanist Giovanni Aurispa carries a complete Greek text of Plato from Constantinople to Venice

1438
Leonardo Bruni, Italian Humanist, translated Aristotles's *Politics* into Italian

from 1453
Greek scholars flee Constantinople after Turkish conquest

1460–1470
Ficino translates Plato

Giorgio Vasari, *Lorenzo de' Medici*, 1534. Oil on wood, 35 x 28 inches (90 x 72 cm). Galleria degli Uffizi, Florence. The Medici family realized their greatest glory and power only in the third generation. Under Lorenzo il Magnifico, Florence reached the peak of its golden age.

1470
The Portuguese discover the Gold Coast
1471
Pope Sixtus IV starts his collection of antique sculptures
1492
Columbus discovers America
1498
Vasco da Gama discovers the sea route to India
1500
Invention of the pocket watch
1512
Nicolaus Copernicus describes the heliocentric solar system in *Commentariolus*
1519
Magellan departs on the first circumnavigation of the globe

alteration to the works themselves or their content. As a result, changes in our understanding of the Renaissance occur only in interpretations of the epoch, and often end up revealing more about the observer than about the historical situation. General agreement has been reached, however, about certain constants in the understanding of the age. Thus, the dramatic contradiction in the Renaissance between a desire for individuality and the suppression of this new seed by a few local tyrants has become a *leitmotif* in Renaissance study.

These regional rulers were only too glad to develop their "private individuality," even at the expense of the rest of the population. At the same time, the mounting social problems in the cities were being exacerbated by tensions between the increasing number of wage-earners, the wealthy urban citizens, and the nobility. At the beginning of the modern era, Italy was a collection of traditional small city-states that had never really recognized one another and attempted to enforce their own wills in a confused and undefined area beyond law. In particular, five powers dominated the course of events: the Republic of Venice, the Pontifical State, the Duchy of Milan, the Republic of Florence, and the Kingdom of Naples. Surrounding these five was a frothy brew of provincial despots who sought to improve their position via sharp practice and intrigue. Whether churchman, general, banker, or nobleman, the origin of the regional rulers varied and basically did not bar access to any to the highest offices. "The need to enlarge oneself, to move oneself at all, is characteristic of all Illegitimates," observed the 19th-century art historian Jakob Burckhardt, describing the variety of despotic personalities who functioned as born strategists, ever calculating the economical, military, and moral capabilities and limitations of their rivals.

Where and when did the Renaissance begin?
In the 15th century, the Alps still largely fulfilled the function described by the poet Francesco Petrarch: A

The Myth of an Epoch

mighty bulwark against the frenzied barbarians beyond. The French kings were engaged in military conflicts with England, and the German emperors were occupied with their own affairs and the conflicts in their realm north of the great mountains. Spared invasion, Italy was able to concentrate entirely on its own political and cultural constellations. It was not until 1494 that Charles VIII of France temporarily involved himself in the complex web of Italian powers. His successor, Louis XII, followed in his footsteps, His efforts in fact largely met with enthusiasm, but Louis could not sustain his position for reasons acutely analyzed by Machiavelli in *The Prince*: "Louis made five mistakes: He destroyed the weak (the lords of the city-states in Romagna), he strengthened the might of a single power in Italy (the pope and his son Cesare Borgia), he drew an extra-territorial foreign power into the country (the Catholic Ferdinand of Spain), he did not establish his residence in Italy, and he did not establish a colony. Even these errors would not have harmed him during his lifetime if he had not made a sixth, namely, taking land away from the Venetians."

Where all of Louis's stratagems and pacts had been inconsequential, Emperor Charles V was more ruthless. His invasion of Italy, culminating in the plundering of the Sack of Rome in 1527, came as a profound shock. This date is also associated with the end of the High Renaissance in Italy. After the brief golden age of art associated with the likes of Leonardo, Raphael, and Giovanni Bellini, by 1520 the signs of the Late Renaissance (also called the Age of Mannerism to emphasize the distinction) had appeared, and by the end of the century the Renaissance flowed seamlessly into the Baroque.

The Italian political situation at the close of the 15th century.

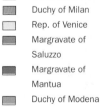

- Duchy of Savoy
- Duchy of Milan
- Rep. of Venice
- Margravate of Saluzzo
- Margravate of Mantua
- Duchy of Modena
- Duchy of Ferrara
- Rep. of Florence
- Republic of Siena

Where and When did the Renaissance Begin?

Many very different dates have been suggested as possible beginnings for the Renaissance: for example the artistic awakening in Tuscany at the beginning of the 15th century; the invention of the printing press in Germany in 1451; the conquest of Constantinople by the Turks in 1453; Columbus's discovery of America in 1492. Each of these dates, however, reveals less about the Renaissance than about the standpoint of the given historian—his or her particular field of interest, or even national and cultural identity.

In the face of this difficulty, it is tempting not to bind the beginning of the Renaissance to a single event but, rather, to see the epoch as a series of innovations, discoveries, and political events rooted in the 13th and 14th centuries, and finally coming to fruition in the 15th century. To understand the Renaissance narrowly as a distinct rebirth of the ancient classical world is to misunderstand it completely. In reality, the continuity between the Middle Ages and the Renaissance is far greater than many of the denigrating remarks of the early Renaissance philosophers would have us believe.

The ancient cultures of Greece and Rome were hardly forgotten or lost during the Middle Ages. Monasteries preserved the writings of such Roman poets and philosophers as Horace, Seneca, and Ovid, while Aristotle had always been highly respected for his moral values. Significant interpretations and translations of antique works, however, were on the whole not undertaken until the Renaissance. Likewise, many of the ancient ruins had not been razed, although, as with the Roman Colosseum, their role as quarries for new construction often overshadowed their aesthetic or historical value. Even the famous ancient Roman architectural treatise by Vitruvius had been copied occasionally in the Middle Ages, although it was not until 1414 that Poggio Bracciolini again brought it to the attention of a new generation of artists who welcomed it with open arms.

Two external circumstances also favored the development of Renaissance culture in Italy. At the beginning of the 14th century, Italy already contained 23 cities, with more than 20,000 inhabitants. Furthermore, the lively trade between the Italian city-states and the culturally significant Greek, Moslem, and Jewish worlds, combined with the worldliness of the Italian metropolises, fostered the highly developed Italian financial system, mirrored today in the common use of words such as "bank" (*banco*). The second crucial element was the absence of external military threat on the Italian peninsula.

Power and art in Renaissance Italy

Initially the Italians were left alone to settle their own military conflicts, allowing a crystalization of power to take place within the peninsula. Around 1400, northern Italy increasingly fell prey to the expansionary fever of Giangaleazzo Visconti, duke of Milan. While many smaller cities capitulated helplessly to his superiority, Milan's threat spurred the Republic of Florence into a new consciousness of its urban identity, which in turn instilled a desire to stand up to the common enemy. Visconti's unexpected death in 1402 came as a redemption for the Florentines and contributed to a new political and cultural self-consciousness in the Tuscan metropolis.

Against this background of newly won confidence and diminished military threat, the Renaissance blossomed in the succeeding decades into an era of rich innovation in all areas of art—in music and literature, as well as in painting, sculpture, and architecture. The early Italian Humanists who had worn the robes of chancellor in the late 14th and early 15th centuries—among them, Coluccio Salutati (1331–1406), Leonardo Bruni (1369–1444), and Gian Francesco Poggio de Guccio Bracciolini (1380–1459)—laid the foundation for this process and eagerly devoted to it all their powers.

These scholars' understanding of classical antiquity became the binding model for the Renaissance; the Middle Ages were designated variously as "barbarian,"

Domenico Ghirlanaio,
The Birth of Mary,
1486–1490. Fresco,
chancel Santa Maria
Novella, Florence.
The old conflict between
disegno (drawing) and
atmosphere, and
between the suppleness
of the figures and their
coloration, was executed
in exemplary fashion by
the painters of Florence
and Venice.

"German," or "Greek" (in disparaging reference to the Byzantine icons of the Eastern Church), and were largely ignored. What mattered to the new way of thinking was to take the human being as the new point of reference and to reflect the human world as naturalistically as possible. The conception of what exactly comprised the naturalistic, however, varied not only from region to region, but also through the course of time. Whereas the Florentine approach to reality in painting consisted largely of the accumulation of a wealth of precisely depicted details, the Venetians of the High Renaissance preferred diffuse color and a perspectival approach to create the illusion of space. Nature and ancient Rome remained common denominators, although even they might be treated in completely different manners.

Jacopo Bassano, *Christ
and the Adultress*, ca.
1450. Oil on canvas, 55
x 88 inches (141 x 225
cm). Museo Bassano del
Grappa.
The diffuse contours
made possible by the
new oil painting that had
been newly adopted in
Venice was developed to
its full potential in the
16th century.

The inventions of the new age

Although Renaissance art is characterized by an appreciable increase in secular pictorial themes, Christian iconography nevertheless remained prevalent throughout the entire Renaissance. The new genres of painting that emerged in the 15th and 16th centuries exemplify this secular trend. Autonomous individual portraits, still lifes, and landscapes acquired legitimacy. Similarly, the geometric construction of central perspective that created depth and integrated the position of the observer into the picture gradually replaced the flat gilded background of the heavenly spheres. The artist now painted less for the glory of God than for the admiration of the public. The human being became the focal point, the measure of all things. The diagram of human proportions, inscribed within a circle and a square, reflected divine harmony and thus the universal laws of creation.

Jacopo de' Barbari, *Still Life with Dead Bird*, 1504. Oil on wood, 20¾ x 16½ inches (52 x 42.4 cm). Alte Pinakothek, Munich

North of the Alps—for the Italians, barbarian lands —the new style developed a character of its own only slightly later. From the North came the technical inventions that were to characterize the culture of the Renaissance: oil painting, wood carving, copper plate etching, and book printing.

The spread of knowledge became a matter of course, revolutionized by Gutenberg's invention of the movable-type printing press. Whereas 45 scribes had once required 22 months to copy 200 books for Cosimo de' Medici, the two German priests who set up Italy's first printing press in the Benedictine cloister of Subiaco in 1465 were able to turn out 12,000 volumes in only five years.

The status of the artist

Parallel with innovations in style and technology during the Renaissance, the social status of the artist also rose. The early Humanists and scholars had come almost entirely from wealthy, respected families, but now those of their sons who wished to become artists faced great hurdles. Artists traditionally belonged to

Leonardo da Vinci, *Diagram of Human Proportions*, illustration for Vetruvius.

Lorenzo Ghiberti, *Self-Portrait in the Frame of the Door of Paradise*, ca. 1447. Bronze, baptistery, Florence.

In the ancient tradition, the liberal arts, or *artes liberales*, were intellectual disciplines, mastery of which was one of the hallmarks of a free man. Around 420 A.D., in his writing on the *Marriage of Mercury and Philology*—an encyclopedic school book that was widely used into the Middle Ages—Martianus Capella identified the liberal arts as seven: arithmetic, dialectic, grammar, rhetoric, geometry, music, and astronomy.

the class of manual workers and were at first simply designated as craftsmen. As such, an artist faced the general social prejudice against mere painters and sculptors. Their activity, dirty and mechanical (an accusation already leveled by Aristotle), was not to be equated with the *artes liberales*. As a craftsman, the artist was considered uneducated, petty-minded, and unenlightened. From Italy to the Netherlands, artists who took themselves seriously attempted to avoid the opprobrium attached to money-grubbing attempts to hock their wares as finished products at fairs or in shops. Instead, "good" artists increasingly established their own studios where they accepted commissions; their names came to stand for style and quality.

It was only in the course of the 15th century that the general image of the artist underwent a transformation, and for the first time individual artists were accorded the highest honors. Thus, Andrea Mantegna was granted the title of count by Pope Innocent III, and Titian even rose to imperial count under Emperor Charles V. The Humanist Cesariano claimed architects were on a level with demigods, and Michelangelo was conferred the epitaph "divine" by both the philosopher Pietro Aretino and the biographer of Renaissance artists, Giorgio Vasari.

Where the financial resources were available—so it is said of Filippino Lippi, Luca Signorelli, and Raphael —many artists of the late 15th and early 16th centuries attempted to evade the stigma of manual work by styling themselves as noble free spirits. Although the nomenclature did nothing to alter their social position, nonetheless, in Italian or Dutch cities where the class of craftsmen was particularly well developed, the conditions for life as an artist were very favorable. In fact, a markedly large number of artists thrived in competition and drew attention to themselves through their innovations and individual styles. Vasari, attempting to find a reasonable explanation for the link between artists, competition, and the resulting artistic quality in his own city, attributed the

phenomenon finally to the "Florentine air."

Because not all artists were willing to confront this pressure to succeed, or precisely because their fame had already transcended regional boundaries, a considerable number of artists betook themselves on journeys to display their work elsewhere. This mobility becomes evident very early: Frescoes by Giotto are to be found in Naples, Rimini, and Padua, the university town within the Venetian sphere of influence where Donatello also worked. The Florentines Verrocchio and Sansovino painted their chief works in Venice, while the Venetian Sebastiano del Piombo went to Rome, where he not only painted but also filled church offices on the side, becoming keeper of the church seal (as expressed by his surname, Piombo, "lead"). Exchanges and mutual inspiration were broad and influential.

Art in princely service

To become an official court painter to one of the princes was the best way for an artist to acquire a secure position. Familiarity, however, often bred contempt, and many a ruler was soon treating the once-prized genius of his hired artist with the same disrespect he showed any other underling. A number of complaints have survived. Mantegna, for example, complained about his life in Mantua, just as Leonardo da Vinci bemoaned conditions in Milan or Benvenuto Cellini his existence at the French court of Francis I. Difficult artistic personalities often collided with the ignorance of their patrons, who at best understood art as evidence of their own social and cultural status—often as mere decoration for opulent festivals and tournaments. It was difficult for an artist in a court position to evade such trivial work. To expend their energies on such ephemeral decorations was naturally

Giorgio Vasari.

According to Vasari, Florentine artists acquired wings through the "critique which is produced in many ways by a great many people, because the air here produces free spirits who are not satisfied with mediocre work…" In addition, he found the city relatively poor, and poverty has been known to foster inventiveness. Finally, "the desire for fame and honor which the air here produces in high concentration in those who produce something perfect" was responsible for the success of Florentine art.

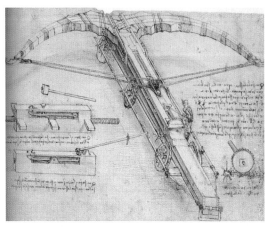

Leonardo da Vinci, *Proposal for a Giant Crossbow*, ca. 1485. Ink over chalk, 8 x 10¾ inches (20.5 x 27.5 cm). Bibliotheca Ambrosiana, Milan.

far less interesting for the artist than creating works for the ages that alone would guarantee enduring fame as a creative genius. Artists were nonetheless well aware of the value of their activity to their patrons, as seen in Leonardo da Vinci's letter of application to the Duke of Milan in 1482: Art stands in the last place. Leonardo recommends himself first as an architect for fortification; next, as a designer of battle wagons, ships, and artillery; in passing he adds: "In peacetime I can construct public and private buildings and I do not think I need to be shy of comparison with any other architect. I know how to lay waterlines,... [I can] do sculpture in marble, bronze, or clay, as well as any other imaginable sort of paintings." At the end he makes a concrete proposal: "The bronze horse that was meant to ensure the undying fame and eternal honor of your father and the reputation of the renowned Sforza dynasty could be taken up once again."

Leonardo da Vinci, *Study for the Sforza Monument* (never built) ca. 1511. Royal Library, Windsor.

The Sforza dynasty, which had been founded only in 1450 by a captain of mercenary troops, certainly was in need of securing respect for itself, because its sole claim to legitimacy rested on its brute military power, as reflected in its name "Sforza," or strength. Leonardo was well aware of this reality. What better symbol for the Sforzas' claim to power but an equestrian memorial to a soldier-leader in the ancient Roman tradition?

Ancient sculpture and architecture were to be found everywhere throughout Italy; the very endurance of the ruins was perceived as an element of their beauty. In this sense, too, the Renaissance saw itself as a revival not merely of ancient, but of eternal values. "Remember... that no memory of us will remain except the walls, which after centuries and millennia will continue to give witness to their makers," Vasari cites the architect Filippo Brunelleschi, who had carefully studied the construction of the Pantheon and other ancient buildings in order to erect the first great dome of modern history for the cathedral of Florence.

Many a local ruler was also interested in preserving his own fame in perpetuity, and turned necessarily to intellectuals and artists. Thus Pisanello, Leon Battista Alberti, Andrea Mantegna, and Guilio Romano were able to make a lasting imprint on the city of Mantua—as did Piero della Francesca and Francesco di Giorgio Martini on the appearance of Urbino, and Cosmè Tura, Lodovico Ariosto, and Torquato Tasso on the culture of Ferrara. Their work proves that even a small city-state might be able to hitch itself for a few decades to the avant-garde of the metropolises that were fitting themslves out with pomp and splendor in all areas during the Renaissance.

Pantheon, Rome, built 118–125 A.D. under Emperor Hadrian.

In Florence, by the middle of the 15th century, the great churches and palaces were being built or were already finished; in Venice, St. Mark's Square essentially acquired its modern face; in Rome, Michelangelo was redesigning first the secular center of the city, the Capitol, and then the sacred, St. Peter's, at the behest of Pope Paul III. Most significantly, architecture was not merely the servant of actual community needs, but rigorously strove beyond existing architectonic models. Thus, the visible demonstration of power by a political and intellectual ruling class took on proportions unimaginable since antiquity.

The heirs of Vitruvius

For Leon Battista Alberti (1404–1472), the first theoretical architect of the modern era, beauty could be defined in terms of mathematical calculation: "The numbers that effect the harmony of voices that the ear finds so extremely pleasant are the same that fill the eyes and the soul with pleasure." Not only do the proportions of the human body obey the laws of harmony, the relations between architectural masses can be derived from the same laws. Alberti cited antiquity to argue that buildings are like living beings and that architecture therefore should adopt its essential principles from nature. The simplest example, he points out, is that just as arms and legs are paired in nature, so the columns of a building should occur only in even numbers.

In *De re aedificatoria* ("On Architecture"), composed around 1450, Alberti reflected the architectonic ideals of the new age by consciously modeling his own work in both form and content on the ancient tract of Vitruvius, *De architectura*, which had been rediscovered in 1414. Although Alberti's work seems not to have been widely known during his lifetime, it exerted a fundamental influence on later generations. Because Vitruvius's illustrations had been lost for centuries, Alberti initially considered it beneath his intellectual dignity to illustrate his own treatise; rather, he felt that his ideas should be so clear and precise as not to require graphic illustration. He maintained his opinion, however, only through the first printing of his work; afterward, until the end of the Renaissance, architecural writings were invariably provided with plans and examples.

Anonymous, *The Ideal City*, late 15th century. Oil on wood, 26½ x 93½ inches (67.5 x 240 cm). Galleria Nazionale delle Marche, Palazzo Ducale, Urbino.

Andrea Palladio, the last great architect of the epoch, still modeled himself after Alberti's ideas. His *Four Books of Architecture* (1570), in fact, are a precise resumé of the humanistic architectural ideals of the waning era.

Many treatises probably originated in a desire to grasp and come to terms with the diffuse writings of Vitruvius and to see them drawn on paper. In practice, the study of Vitruvius was increasingly accompanied by concrete and detailed attention to the surviving Roman buildings, so that theory and reality supported each other, albeit not always without contradiction. Two centuries later, the German writer Goethe probably expressed the frustration experienced by many Renaisance architects in reading Vitruvius's difficult descriptions: "This folio is dead weight in my luggage, just as the study is in my brain... . Vitruvius is not easy to read; the book itself is unclearly written and requires critical study" (*Italian Journey*, October 12, 1786).

Sacred architecture

Especially in the area of church construction, architects of the early Renaissance attempted to model themselves on ancient temples; Alberti even used the term "temple" to refer to sacred Christian buildings.

As a practicing architect, Alberti made his debut with the renovation of the medieval church of San Francesco in Rimini. He covered the original church with a white stone mantle. On the sides of the building, barrel-domed niches built into the mantle offered a place for sarcophagi. Furthermore, the theme of the arches is picked up once more by the building's facade (which, however, remained unfinished), whose clear details relate proportionally to the basic square structure of the building. As the burial church for the Malatesta family, the building has entered architectural history as the Tempio Malatestiano.

Leon Battista Alberti, Facade, Tempio Malatestiano, begun after 1453/1468 (incomplete). San Francesco, Rimini.

In the age of Alberti, however, research into classical antiquity was not yet sufficiently advanced to yield a precise picture of either the functions or the construction dates of surviving ancient buildings and ruins. As a result, many antique secular buildings were mistaken for temples; on the other hand, some sacred buildings that in fact dated from a later period, such as the San Stefano Rotondo and the baptistery in Florence, were assumed to be ancient buildings that had been adapted by the Christian cult for its services. In reality, the only ancient element in the baptistery is its marble paneling, which was taken from Roman ruins. The surface of geometric patterns that characterize the building is not of antique origin, but was rather a creation of the so-called pre-Renaissance of the 12th century. But, because no questions were raised about its supposed antique origin, Renaissance architects drew "antique" inspiration from the baptistery for the facade of Santa Maria Novella with a clean conscience. Thus, "[A] building whose interior emphasizes the full austerity of the Dominican spirit was given a facade from which all austerity has been removed, a facade that desires nothing but to hold up its noble surface, softly differentiated by intarsia, to the setting sun." (Paul Schubring, 1923)

Baptistery, 1060–1150, Florence.

If architectural practice occasionally made such errors, they were balanced out by the precision of the theoretical approach to church construction, as is clear from Alberti's seventh book: Temples must be elevated and free-standing, and sport both a columned front and an arched roof. Furthermore, white is the fitting color for God, and the interior design must be simple. The best decoration, therefore, consists of sculptures, also white, that can be enhanced with ornaments of philosophical clarity.

Facade of the Santa Maria Novella, completed by Leon Battista Alberti, 1456–1478, Florence.

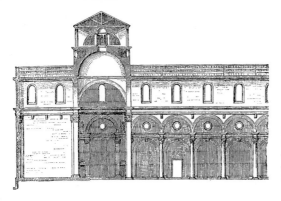

Filippo Brunelleschi, San Lorenzo, cut-away diagram of wall of the central nave, 1432–1425. Florence.

According to the humanist Luca Pacioli, only in a well-shaped space that corresponded to these harmonies could the effect of a church service develop fully. The spatial organization of the San Lorenzo Basilica in Florence (begun in 1421) bespoke clarity and human proportions, and accepted many of these requirements from the start.

The Renaissance was an era in which the Humanists, having steeped themselves in both theory and philosophy, threw themselves enthusiastically into debates about the relative values of the *vita activa* and the *vita contemplativa*. Where Coluccio Salutati defended communal life over a meditative flight from the world, Leon Battista Alberti—in the *Disputationes camaldulenses* transcribed by Cristoforo Landino—at first laid weight on the long-lasting values of contemplation; later, however, Alberti, too, came to value the man who was able to unite both sides harmonically within himself.

Alberti exhibited personally an ideal combination of both approaches. As a broadly educated scholar, sportsman and artist, he was the first *uomo universale* of modern history. By the mid-15th century, in addition to his architectural treatise, he had written tracts on painting (*Della pittura*), love—how to sustain it and how to renounce it (*Dei fira / Ecaton fira*), the advantages and disadvantages of writing as a career (*De commodis literarum arque incommodis*), household life (*Della famiglia*), and other questions of Humanism (*Theogenius, Momus*). In later years, he was active as an architect himself.

Alberti rarely made a personal appearance at the construction site of his own buildings; instead he allowed most of his commissions to be carried out by a local building master who worked from Alberti's plans. Thus, even in the role of construction engineer, Alberti could maintain the role of the noble spirit and theoretician who did not descend to dirty his hands at the building site. His discriminating approach played a significant role in the increasing separation between planning and construction, and ultimately in defining the role of the architect.

left:
Leon Battista Alberti, San Andrea, cornerstone laid 1472; completed 1494. Facade with portico, Mantua. Alberti's interest in antiquity found expression in the motif of the triumphal arch that is part of the church facade.

right:
Leon Battista Alberti, San Andrea. Interior view, Mantua.

After the Tempio Malatestiano, the San Andrea church in Mantua reflected most powerfully the ideals and the compromises demanded by actual construction. The facade of the church is based on a triumphal arch symbolizing the *Ecclesia triumphans*, or the Church Victorius. Precisely in an era of crisis, in which Byzantium was conquered by the Turks, every possible propagandistic demonstration of power was useful. The nave draws from the architecture of the ancient thermal baths and presents a harmonious integration of the whole down to the breadth of a pilaster based on a common denominator.

The waning 15th century produced another series of broadly noteworthy writings on architecture, in particular those of the sculptor and architect Francesco de Giorgio Martini (1439–1501/02). Beyond the tropes of Humanistic education, Martini's work provides concrete directions for almost all aspects of construction and is further enriched by well-considered designs for every architectural requirement. In addition, it reveals an earnest attempt to come to terms with the heritage of Vitruvius.

Francesco di Giorgio Martini (attributed), *Architectural View*, ca. 1477. Oil on wood, 48⅜ x 91¼ inches (124 x 234 cm). Gemälde-galerie, Berlin.

Rome and Venice

In the 16th century, a new "age of heathenry in Italian architecture" (Erich Hubala) developed, based on ongoing archaeological research and critical consideration of early Renaissance studies.

Donato Bramante, Tempietto, San Pietro in Montorio, ca. 1502–1510, Rome.

The great age of Florentine architecture came to an end—even if Michalangelo was once more to set new standards with his *Biblioteca aurentiana*. With the decline of Florence, two other metropolises now took the initiative: In Rome, Donato Bramante (Donato d'Angelo Lazzari, 1444–1514), who had maintained close contact with Leonardo da Vinci in Milan, came to define architectural taste at the beginning of the century with his Tempietto as well as his designs for the rebuilding of St. Peter's (the foundation stone was laid in 1506). In addition,

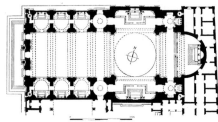

Giacomo da Vignola,
Il Gesù, floorplan,
1568–1573, Rome.

Bramante's colleague, Giacomo da Vignola (1507–1573), developed the prototype of an ideal union of a centrally organized building that was combined with a long nave in the Jesuit church Il Gesù.

Meanwhile, in Veneto (in northeastern Italy), Andrea Palladio (1508–1580) became the standard bearer among architects with his construction of villas. Originally a simple stonemason, Palladio was discovered and fostered by the poet Giangiorgio Trissino, and in the Humanistic atmosphere, he developed into one of the most important theoreticians and innovators of his time. Critical interest in antiquity was especially strong in the area around Venice—Padua boasted the most important of the 13 Italian universities, and Veneto the largest contingent of Humanists.

Palladio's architectural treatise, published in 1570, exerted as powerful an influence on the next three centuries of European and American architecture as the Roman buildings of Bramante, Vignola, and Michelangelo. In England, a movement clearly based on Palladian's work developed. The first of the four books of the treatise dealt with the principles of architecture, materials, orders of columns, and parts of buildings; the second presented antique buildings as well as Palladio's own; the third dealt with streets, bridges, piazzas, open colonnades, and basilicas; and the final part dealt with temples.

Andrea Palladio,
Bramante's
Tempietto.
Illustration from
his treatise.

Prior to the publication of Palladio's study, Sebastiano Serlio (1475–1554/55) had written an architectural treatise divided into seven books that addressed geometry, perspective, antiquities, five building styles, temples, fifty portal designs, and various types of houses. Palladio had boldly placed his designs alongside the ancient models; Serlio, in contrast, considered it a great honor for an architect like Bramante to treat his own works and ancient works in the same chapter.

Whereas Palladio's clear, spare prose writings have generally been praised as an extraordinary achievement, history has tended to characterize Serlio as small-minded. "Serlio offends against not only all of Vitruvius's rules but also good taste in his sixth book when he sets out to sketch fifty different portals, and necessarily has to descend to bizarre and ugly shapes," complained Otto Stein in 1914, following in the footsteps of the influential Renaissance scholar Jakob Burckhardt, whose taste was so uncompromisingly shaped by antique ideals that any deviation was viewed as an error of taste.

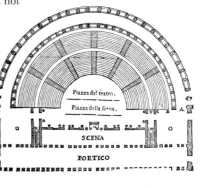

Sebastiano Serlio, Antique Theater. Illustration from his treatise.

"Remember," wrote Palladio, sharing here in Serlio's judgment, "that Bramante was the first to bring the good and beautiful architecture to light–that which had been hidden since ancient times." Such a statement seems almost to erase the entire architectural achievement of the 15th century. For Palladio, the history of "good"—that is, classically oriented—architecture resumed only during the pontificat of Julius II, and advanced in the works of Michelangelo, Sansovino, Peruzzi, Sangallo, and similar masters.

When one recalls that, in 1436, Leonardo Bruni had described Petrarch as the first "to whom such discernment was given to recognize the charm of the antique and to bring it out of forgetfulness, out of the twilight, into life once more," and that Alberti was simultaneously being celebrated by his Florentine friends as the rediscoverer of antiquity, the extreme variety and divergence of perceptions and evaluations of the Renaissance championed by its leading personalities become abundantly clear.

The view from Mount Ventoux

When Francesco Petrarch died in 1374, he left behind
an imaginary conversation with St. Augustine entitled
Secretum, in which he described the weaknesses and
risability of his own character. The work culminated in
the maxim, "Reflect upon yourself!" This introspection
by the first self-analyst of the modern world is typical of
one side of Petrarch, and it is no wonder that the first
surviving picture of the personal experiences of an
artist stem precisely from this poet of Arezzo. When
Pertrach desired a longer view, he had only to climb
Mount Ventoux near Vaucluse. The confusion and
enthusiasm engendered in him by the wonderful
panorama characterize an entirely new way of looking
at the world. But even on the mountain peak, Petrarch
remembered his Augustine: The ascent of the
mountain was but a symbol of the weary vanity of
earthly existence.

In his joy in the perception of nature, however,
Petrarch had made an important historical step that
liberated the arts and fostered the development of an
interest in the physical reality of the world. To see the
world not merely as a vale of tears, as Pope Innocent
III had denigrated it in his encyclical *De comtempto
mundi* ("On the Contempt of the World"), but instead
as a wondrous creation of God, signified a change of

Nardo di Cione, *The Last
Judgment* (detail),
1354–1357. Fresco,
Cappella Strozzi, Santa
Maria Novella, Florence.

Nicola Pisano, *Birth of Christ*, 1259–1260. Marble chancel, baptistery, Pisa.
The variety of positions, gestures, characters, and clothing studies in Pisano's scenes results in a seamless massing of human figures, animals, and architectural shapes. These are never merely flat and ornamental; rather they enrich one another with sophisticated layering and overlapping that seems to create a free-standing sculptural effect for individual figures in the foreground.

attitude that would soon find expression in painting and sculpture.

Nature and antiquity

Many different personalites and influences contributed to the growth of this new naturalism. Nicola Pisano (ca. 1225–1280) and his son Giovanni (1245/50–ca. 1315) developed a style that combined detailed observation of nature with an unprejudiced appreciation of the antique. As they worked on the pulpits in the cathedral (1260) and baptistery (1311) in Pisa, they kept the old Roman sarcophagi constantly within view—with

1348
First of the great European plague epidemics
1348–53
Giovanni Boccaccio writes the *Decamerone*, the first novel of modern times, composed of 100 short stories.

Panofsky on Petrarch
While all Christian thinkers before him had interpreted history [...] as a continual progress from heathen darkness to the light that was Christ, [...] Petrarch understood the epoch, in which "the name of Christ was adored in Rome and praised by the Roman emperors," as the beginning of the "dim" age of decline and darkening, while the preceding era—for him, simply the time of Rome and its kings, the Republic, and the emperors—as a time of fame and light. He felt he had been born too early to see the new day whose dawning he sensed; "but for you," he wrote in his famous poem *Africa*, penned in 1338, one year after his first trip to Rome, "for you, if you outlive me by many years, as I hope and wish with all my soul, a better time is imminent; the slumber of forgetfulness will not last forever. Once the darkness is destroyed, our grandchildren will move in the clear light of the past."
Petrarch was too good a Christian not to be aware of—at least from time to time—that this idea of classical antiquity as an era of "pure light" and, on the other hand, of the era since the christening of Constantine the Great as an era of dark ignorance would lead to a complete reversal of generally accepted values.
From: Erwin Panofsky, *Renaissance and Renascences in Western Art*, 1960.

tangible effect: On the marble relief depicting the birth of Christ on the pulpit of the baptistery, the figure of Mary obviously derives from either a Roman sarcophagus or an Etruscan urn.

The new wealth of imagery, together with the rich decoration of the pulpits, is a direct reaction to the historical religious events and developments of the first half of the 13th century. In the figures of St. Dominic (1170–1221) and St. Francis (1181/82–1226), there appear on the Italian scene two strong personalities, both of whom founded new monastic orders and infused new meaning and life into the increasingly ossified religious traditions of their age.

The imaginative and easily visualized preachings of the Franciscans in particular evoked an immediate response in the arts—and no artist seemed more able to take advantage of the region's multicultural avant-garde than Nicola Pisano, who had come to Pisa from Apuleia in the south of Italy.

In southern Italy the German Staufer emperor Frederick II had established both a centralized state and a culture that radically surpassed the moral and stylistic conventions of his age. His successes, however, had not only earned him a reputation as the first modern emperor, but also set him into a permanent conflict with Pope Gregory IX, who considered Frederick to be the anti-Christ incarnate. In spite of the pope's antagonism, Frederick's court continued to burst with Norman soldiers and Arabic scholars, heathens and Christians, bringing together people from a broad range of backgrounds. All these influences came together in Nicola Pisano.

Giotto, *The Kiss of Judas*, 1304–1306. Fresco, 78 x 72 inches (200 x 185 cm). Cappella degli Scrovegni all'Arena, Padua.

Giotto (1266?–1337)

The figures of Giotto's painting are, like the Pisanos', rooted in the new realistic world. The Florentine painter, however, limited himself in his work far more to depicting only the persons and objects that were necessary to tell the story of his pictures. He thus achieved an intellectual clarity and serenity that stands in direct opposition to the overflowing richness of the work of the Pisanos.

Giotto, *Flagellation (Coronation with Thorns)*, 1304–1306. Fresco, 78 x 72 inches (200 x 185 cm). Cappella degli Scrovegni all'Arena, Padua.
"With Giotto, painting achieved a significance, a weight and a dignity that it had never before possessed. It was in painting that something fundamentally new, the change from the medieval world to a new age, occurred. Neither with its architecture nor with sculpture did Italy enter the field of Western art as an equal, but with the frescos of the Arena."
Theodor Hetzer, *Giotto*, 1941.

Giotto's studies of nature fascinated the poet Giovanni Boccaccio, who wrote that the painter "possessed a spirit of such superiority that, among all that Mother Nature has produced under the heavens, there was not a single thing that he could not illustrate with stylus and brush so that it would seem to be the object itself; and his work did not seem to be a picture of an object, but the object itself, so that it often happened that the viewer of his works might be confused by the facial expression of the figure, and that which seemed to be reality was only what had been painted." This statement already introduces the standard Renaissance formula of appreciation for the amazing nearness to nature—for the perfect imitation, and even a contest with nature—that was to be applied for many purposes over the ensuing 200 years. Even among artists separated from each other by a century, comparisons of the praise of Giotto's work with the high evaluation accorded the works of Masaccio (by Landino, for example) and of Leonardo (by Vasari) make it clear that such praise is easily applied at will, but objectively says almost nothing about the specific quality of the art in question. What seems evident in all three artists is their primary orientation toward nature as a model and their rejection of traditional assumptions.

An anecdote that has been a part of art history ever since it was recorded by Lorenzo Ghiberti illustrates the birth of the new Renaissance style: Giotto, when he was just a shepherd boy, sat beside a highway drawing one of his sheep when the painter Giovanni Cimabue happened to pass by. Recognizing the boy's potential, Cimabue immediately took Giotto with him to be an apprentice in his workshop.

The Arena Chapel in Padua, named after the ancient Roman arena it stands next to, marks a milestone in the Renaissance journey away from the heavenly spheres. Giotto was hired by Erminio Scrovegni from 1304 to 1306 to paint the chapel—a commission that seemed tantamount to blasphemy because the rich money-lender Scrovegni had merely been one of the financiers of the chapel and had proceeded to appropriate the edifice as a family chapel. The problem was not only usury, for which his family was infamous (and for which his father was left to stew in Dante's *Inferno*), but the Arena Chapel was considered far too large to be a mere family memorial chapel.

But now, with the expert advice of a Franciscan friar, Scrovegni developed an iconographic theme for the

The divine circle as the sign of genius

The pope sent a courtier though the studios of Tuscany in search of artists for the Vatican. After the messenger had gathered samples from the other artists of Florence, he came to Giotto and demanded a sample of his work. "Giotto, who was very polite, took up a piece of paper and a brush with red paint and, laying his arm on the side to act as a compass, drew with the motion of his hand a circle so clear and exact that he was amazed; he bowed to the courtier and said, 'There. You have your drawing.' In horror the courtier asked, 'Is that all you're giving me?' 'It's enough, and even too much,' came the reply. 'Send it along with the others you've gathered, and you will see whether it is recognized.' The messenger, who saw well enough that he wasn't likely to be given anything else, went away unhappily..."

The self-confidence of the artist who sent the pope nothing but a circle was rewarded, for the Vatican had a good understanding of art and recognized "how much Giotto surpassed the painters of his age."

The veracity of this anecdote preserved by Vasari is not the key issue; its message is nonetheless clear. After "good painting" and drawing had been thoroughly destroyed, it was an act of "heavenly grace" that the miracle of Giotto appeared. Humankind had driven art into destruction, and Giotto was a gift from Heaven, which always brings about resurrection. Heaven awakened him to life, and even the Vatican immediately recognized this divine sign.

interior that could not be outdone for its Christian morality. On the foundation, *The Virtues and Vices* are portrayed in *grisaille*, a gray-on-gray technique, between the painted marble panels. Over them, displayed in three rows, is the story of the life of Jesus and Mary; on the portal wall is the Last Judgment; and on the ceiling of the prophetical roof, no lesser figures than Mary, John the Baptist, and God the Father. The cycle derives variously from biblical sources, the *Legenda aurea* ("Golden Legend") of Jacobus de Voragine, and the newly published Franciscan texts, *Meditationes vitae Christi* and *Arbor vitae crucifixae Jesu*.

The carefully thought out theological structure of the room is as innovative as its painterly execution. Giotto's figures are at home in their earthly landscape; they no longer float in the usual shimmering golden background, but possess weight and even a certain individuality. In his model-like architecture, Giotto tried to create the illusion of space, and his observation of nature, already evident in the anecdote of his meeting with Cimabue, was reflected in his naturalistic representations of animals. For the biographer Vasari, Giotto was the father of modern painting, the initiator of a new departure into true art.

Giotto's high reputation during his lifetime led to his appointment as architect for the cathedral in Florence. In this capacity, he laid the foundation stones for the campanile in his last years.

Simone Martini (1284–1344) and Ambrogio Lorenzetti (late 13th century–ca. 1348)

The city of Siena, the great rival of Florence, experienced its own golden age in the 14th century, in which fundamental contributions to the history of art were made. Three figures stand out in particular: Ambrogio and Pietro Lorenzetti, and Simone Martini.

In 1316, Martini finished a fresco in the Palazzo Pubblico—a *Maestà* (or virgin), reminiscent of a tapestry in its design. The work was inspired by the *Maestà* that Duccio had created for the Siena cathedral

Simone Martini, *Maestà*, 1315. Fresco, 300 x 380 inches (763 x 970 cm). Palazzo Pubblico, Siena.
The throned Madonna turns toward Jesus, who is standing on her knee, blessing the assembly. They are surrounded by the sacred train of saints and angels.

in 1311, a monumental building that, according to legend, had been built over the foundation of a temple to Minerva, the goddess of wisdom. Martini, however, not only brought religion to the secular Palazzo Pubblico, but also imported the figure of Minerva/Sapientia. Under the canopy adorned with the coat of arms of the city-state of Siena, Mary sits enthroned as a reigning queen amid her assembled court—and in fact, she was only in the city hall "on a visit," because her real throne remained, of course, in the cathedral.

Already in 1317, a decade before Giotto, Simone Martini was appointed court painter to King Robert of Naples; he later also contributed to the church of St. Francis in Assisi. In 1328, after returning to Siena, he painted the portrait of the general Guidoriccio da Fogliano, who had captured the forts of Montemassi and Sassoforte for Siena, on the wall opposite the *Maestà*. In the center foreground of the fresco, the mounted conquerer stands alone in profile. The first landscape painting in Italian art, containing both

Simone Martini, *Guidoriccio da Fogliano at the Siege of Montemassi*, 1328. Fresco, 132½ x 377½ inches (340 x 968 cm). Palazzo Pubblico, Siena.

Ambrogio Lorenzetti, *The Allegory of Good Goverment* (detail), 1337–1339. Fresco, 115½ x 545 inches (296 x 1398 cm), Palazzo Pubblico, Siena.

besieged fortresses, surrounds him like a prospect. In Martini's hands, the horseman becomes a monument to worldly, military power. He embodies the fortunate martial artist and seems to be a consciously conceived counterimage to the religious power of the mother of God portrayed on the other side of the room. After all, not only faith but also deeds were necessary to secure the largely independent future of the commonwealth of the city-state.

After the departure of the official state artist Simone Martini, who was called to the court of Pope Benedict XXIII in Avignon in 1336, an increasing proportion of the commissioned artworks in Siena fell to the Lorenzetti brothers.

The Good and Bad Government, commissioned by the administration of Siena for Ambrogio Lorenzetti to paint before their very eyes, remains today an unsurpassed source of information for scholars of the customs and traditions, fashions and ideals, politics and philosophy of the times. In this allegory, Lorenzetti depicts the life of a late medieval city set in the midst of

Ambrogio Lorenzetti, *The Results of Good Government* (detail), ca. 1337–1339. Fresco, 93½ x 54½ inches (240 x 140 cm). Palazzo Pubblico, Siena. With his brush, Lorenzetti designed an ideal city based on virtue.

35

Altichiero da Zevio (1320/30–after 1384), *Crucifixion*, ca. 1379–1384. Fresco, Oratorio di San Giorgio, Padua.

the familiar landscape surrounding Siena. This innovative presentation is the unique historical witness of a social organism in which every person seems to have his or her appointed place.

The head of the hall is commanded by *The Good Government*, while the left is decorated with *The Bad Government* and its consequences. In the party of the good, Lorenzetti included the cardinal virtues, seated on their governmental benches: Strength (*Fortitudo*), Prudence (*Prudentia*), Temperence (*Temperentia*), Justice (*Justitia*), Peace (*Pax*), and Magnanimity (*Magnanimitas*). The ruler, who is the personification of the Sienese community, wears the letters C(ommune), S(enarum), C(ivitas), and V(irginis), while around him hover the Christian virtures of Faith (*Fides*), Hope (*Spes*), and Charity (*Caritas*). In his closed hand, the ruler bears a scepter—but also a rope which binds him, on one end, to the 24 councilmen standing before his throne and, on the other end, passes through the hand of Harmony (*Concordia*), carrying a carpenter's plane that makes all equal and continues directly to the Scales of Justice, above which Wisdom hovers.

The next fresco depicts the effects that can be attributed to such intelligent goverment: A blooming city and landscpe filled with happy and bustling activity, including peasants at work in the fields, young girls dancing in the streets, and a noble hunting party riding past the city gate. Above the scene sails the lightly clad figure of *Securitas*, her braids flying in the wind, holding a small admonitory gallows and a script in verse guaranteeing a life without fear under the protection of justice.

Giotto, the Pisanis, the Lorenzettis, and Martini stand as the seminal figures at the beginning of the promising new perception of reality that marked the Renaissance. Their work fascinated and influenced that of succeeding artists well into the following century.

Lorenzo (1374–1420) and Giacomo Salimbeni, *Johannes Baptizes* (detail), 1416. Fresco, Oratorio di San Giovanni, Urbino.
In the area around Tuscany, stylistic innovations were able to to make quick headway and found important representatives in artists such as Altichiero da Zevio, the founder of the Old Veronese school of painting, and Giacomo Salimbeni in the provinces.

International Gothic

Around the year 1400, the so-called International Style, a relatively unified language of forms, developed within European art. The new style also contributed in a way to the hesitating secularization of art, because the decisive impulses arose less from the church than from the princely courts in Paris, Prague, and Milan. The complex and intertwined family connections among the ruling houses, particularly the relation of the Bohemian court to the French—but also the marriage of Galeazzo Visconti, Duke of Milan, to the sister of Count Amadeus VI of Savoy—led to a the increasing dissemination of art, especially of relatively easily transportable book illuminations.

The International Style, characterized by delicate figures, graceful architectural shapes, soft drapings, and occasionally a decorative gold background, became very popular among the emerging bourgeois society. Unlike most medieval figures, those of the new style posed in stances of romantic thoughtfulness or cultivated conversation, as in the altarpiece *Annunciation and Visitation* by Melchior Broderlam (active 1381–ca. 1409). As always, Christian themes claim the foreground of the painting, but the rich ornamentation and elegant clothing import the familiar images of Christ's Passion, the devotional pictures, and representations of saints and of Vanity into the realm of fashionable modernity.

Melchior Broederlam, *Annunciation and Visitation* (left panel of an altarpiece), 1394–1399. Tempera on wood, 63 x 51 inches (162 x 130 cm). Museé des Beaux-Arts, Dijon.

The Limburg Brothers, *Les Très Riches Hures du duc de Berry*, Month of October, ca. 1415. 11½ x 8¼ inches (29 x 21 cm). Musée Condé, Chantilly.
The picture for October portrays a peasant at work—and is the first figure in the history of art to cast a shadow.

In a finely proportioned study bordering on a small walled garden (a *hortus conclusus*, representing Paradise), an elegant Mary greets the rosy-cheeked Gabriel as the golden breath of God flows into her. In the right half of the picture, Mary meets Elizabeth, mother of John the Baptist. This meeting of the two pregnant women before a barren mountain landscape—drawn from the story in the Gospel of Luke—may be a reference to the power of divine fruitfulness in the sterility of earthly existence. Gabriel and Elizabeth both confirm Mary's honored role as the mother of God, and thus become the original authorities within the expanding cult of the Virgin Mary.

A high point in courtly artisitic creativity is the famed "Book of Hours," *Les Très Riches Heures du duc de Berry*, which was designed by the Limburg brothers (active 1375 and 1385/1416). Unfortunately, both the project's patron and the artists seem to have died in the plague epidemic of 1416 before the book could be completed. A full-page miniature depicting contemporary life, as well as the signs of the zodiac, is devoted to each calendar month. These detailed scenes are among the earliest examples of genre painting. Direct reference to the patron of the work, along with his family members and castles, honor the book's commissioner.

Already in the 15th century, the art of the illuminated manuscript possessed the charming antique flair of a genre that has outlived itself, a fact that the gleaming examples of the age must not be allowed to obscure. The invention of the printing press finally sealed the fate of manuscript illumination.

The International Style continued to be prevalent in Italy, represented by Gentile da Fabriano (ca. 1370–1427), teacher of Jacopo Bellini, and Lorenzo Monaco (ca. 1370–ca. 1425), among others. Whereas Lorenzo was one of the few Sienese who was able to adapt himself artistically to the atmosphere of Florence, Gentile led a more peripatetic life. He played a role in the decoration of the Doge's Palace in Venice, worked as court painter to the Malatesta in Brescia, and additionally was active in Florence, Siena, Orvieto, and in the Vatican for Pope Martin V.

Lorenzo Monaco, *Annunciation*, 1410–1415. Tempera on wood, 50¾ x 89¾ inches (130 x 230 cm). San Trinità, Florence.

It was the works of the Florentine sculptor Lorenzo Ghiberti and of the Dominican Fra Angelico that kept the graceful poetry of the Late Gothic alive. Ghiberti, who was trained as a goldsmith, was commissioned to create a pair of bronze doors for the baptistery in Florence, which became the religious focus of the city's life. Fra Angelico, who became prior of the Monastery of San Marco in Florence in 1445, was a great master of landscape and light, and highly respected in both Florence and Rome.

Gentile da Fabriano, *Adoration of the Magi*, 1423. Tempera on wood, 117 x 127 inches (300 x 325 cm). Galleria degli Uffizi, Florence. In the work of Gentile da Fabriano, the joy in the variety of ornament and content that characterizes the International Gothic style is clear. An overloaded decoration, engraved applications of gold leaf, and symbolic references unite with a naturalistic representation of animals and faces. The religious content of the picture pales in comparison to the splendor of the treatment of the materials.

1356
The Golden Bull, the basic imperial law of Charles IV; it formed the constitution of the German Empire until 1806

1378–1417
Great Western Schism; antipopes in Avignon and Rome

1381
Venice wins sea war against Genoa and controls trade with the Orient

1385–1402
Reign of Giangaleazzo Visconti as duke of Milan

1387
Geoffrey Chaucer writes the *Canterbury Tales*, cornerstone of modern English literature

1389
Turks defeat the Serbs in the Battle of the Blackbird Field

1395
Visconti family in Milan receives the title of duke

1406
Florence annexes Pisa

1410–1437
Sigismund, King of Hungary, becomes emperor of the Roman-German empire

1414–1418
Council of Constance; election of Pope Martin V in 1417

1415
Johann Hus, Czech reformer, burned as heretic

1434–1464
Cosimo de' Medici returns to Florence from exile and assumes power

The first generation

By the end of the medieval period, the concrete evidence of classical antiquity consisted chiefly of a number of more—or less—imposing ruins and a few surviving literary works. This dearth of evidence meant that the past came to serve as an ideal *tabula rasa* on which Renaissance thinkers could project their own ideas of the glory of the ancient world. For artists, however, the situation was different. Because no exemplars of antique painting seem to have survived, Renaissance painters looked back to Pisano, Giotto, and Duccio for their roots—in other words, they turned to the local medieval tradition of Tuscany.

At the beginning of the 15th century, Florence saw the rise of a new group of artists, celebrated by Leon Battista Alberti in his treatise on painting (published in 1435): "At one and the same time I was constantly amazed and saddened at the present neglect—in fact, the almost total decay—of the many glorious and divine arts and sciences that were cultivated in antiquity and which we know about both from the works that have survived and from history: Such painters, sculptors, architects, musicians, geometricians, orators, soothsayers and similar noble and admirable spirits are very hard to find nowadays." Alberti continues: "After a long exile (during which we matured), I returned again to our own fatherland, which surpasses all others, and I came to understand that many artists, but particularly you, Filippo [Brunelleschi], and our close friend, the sculptor Donato [Donatello], as well as the others, Cencio [Ghiberti] Luca [della Robbia] and Masaccio, possess a living spirit that is capable of every glorious deed—a spirit that must not be accounted at all inferior to that of the old days, however great and famous this spirit might have been in these arts."

Filippo Brunelleschi, the eldest of these five Florentine masters, was responsible for working out the proper construction of central, or single-point, perspective, a development that was first effectively employed by his younger collegue Masaccio. Although

Brunelleschi was active as both a painter and a sculptor, it was as an architect that he secured his place in art history. It is nonetheless significant that he seriously pursued all three of the graphic arts and himself understood all three as modes of expression of a single great idea.

Brunelleschi was moreover concerned with the improvement of the status of the artist, for as the son of a notary, he was not content to be classified as a mere craftsman. Although two-thirds of the artists of the Renaissance period rose from the ranks of the handworking trades, some of the most important innovators emerged from the higher social classes. Masaccio, like Brunelleschi, was the son of a notary, while Donatello was a scion of the impoverished but noble Bardi family. In this social milieu, an understanding of the self prevailed that was not willing to accept social decline as the price for being an artist.

Through architecture, Brunelleschi acquired status in a roundabout way. Although painters and sculptors were generally considered artisans into the 15th century, architecture was clearly based on the *artes liberales*, in particular on the "free arts" of geometry and arithmetic, and could therefore be regarded as their equal. Beyond the *artes liberales*, the so-called *studia humanitatis*, that is, the study of grammar, literature, rhetoric, history, and philosophy, further rounded out and embellished the student. To be accepted as equals in the select circle of the arts in spite of the manual nature of their work increasingly became the goal of painters, sculptors, and architects.

Luca della Robbia (1399/1400–1482), *Cantoria* (detail), ca. 1431–38. Marble, 38½ x 37 inches (99 x 95 cm.), total size 128 x 218½ inches (328 x 560 cm). Museo dell'Opera del Duomo, Florence.
The sign hanging in front of the thriving workshop of della Robbias was of the same polychrome majolica reliefs with which he decorated Tuscany. In competition with Donatello's *Chancelry Singers* in the cathedral of Florence, della Robbia created a *Cantoria* that attempted to unite the ancient ideal with Christian iconography—even in such details as the dancing putti, which resemble the figure of Eros.

1441
Portugal begins the slave trade
1444
Death of Humanist Leonardo Bruni, the biographer of Dante, Petrarch, and Boccaccio; Cosimo de' Medici founds the public library of San Marco in Florence
1447
Pope Nicolas V establishes the Vatican Library
ca. 1450
Ghiberti's *Commentarii*, first Italian treatise on art history

It is interesting to observe how the image of the artist changed in the course of a single generation. In his treatise on art, the painter Cennino Cennini (ca. 1370–early 15th century) describes his ideal of education for a young artist: "You must understand that it takes time to learn … things. First, it will take at least a year to become good at drawing on a small panel; afterwards you must stand at the side of the master for six years in the workshop until you have learned all the facets belonging to our art. Then you start to prepare the paints, to cook the glue-watercolors, to paint plaster, and to learn how to prepare a plaster base, to emboss it, and to engrave, to gild, and to granulate. And then the practical experiments in painting—using acids in decorating, creating golden garments, becoming adept at painting murals—require another six years—and you must keep at it constantly, on both holidays and workdays."

In *Della pittura* (1435), the first theoretical treatise on painting in modern times, Alberti defends the social status of the artist by citing the antique custom of instructing free-born sons in painting as well as geometry and music in order to provide them with the basis for a good and happy life. Earlier, the Greeks had also valued painting so highly, Alberti observes, that they even forbade it being taught to slaves: "And here they did right, for the art of painting has always been something for liberal-minded spirits (*liberale ingengni*) and the worthiest nobles (*omini nobili dignitissima*)."

As the taste for art developed, and its consumers developed more and more into connoisseurs, it was only natural that increased artistry and expertise were required of the painter. As Alberti had demanded, the painter had to study the liberal arts, especially geometry, in

Filippo Brunelleschi, Cathedral Dome, 1420–1436. Florence.

order to perfect his art. To Alberti, the manual tasks such as the painting of plaster or the laborious preparation of paints were no longer considered to be demeaning hurdles that the painter had to overcome on his way to perfection.

Filippo Brunelleschi, San Spirito, nave, begun mid-15th century. Florence.

Filippo Brunelleschi (1377–1446)

The first great architectural accomplishment of the Renaissance was the construction of the dome of the Cathedral of Florence. Without using a weight-bearing scaffold, Brunelleschi managed to construct a two-shelled self-supporting dome that not only could compete with the venerable churches in Siena and Pisa, but that also incorporated ancient Roman architectural principles. Brunelleschi had already unveiled his model in 1418. However, it required a full two decades to raise the mighty structure, which still dominates the skyline of Florence and constitutes the last of the three great stages in the logical and harmonious design of the cathedral plaza: the baptisterium (1060–1150), the campanile (started 1334), and the dome (from 1420).

Brunelleschi gave his churches the clarity of a pure geometrical architecture and returned once more to the encrusted marble walls that had been favored in the proto-Renaissance. Almost as if he wished to be the sole creator of the building and all its effects, Brunelleschi avoided any decoration with frescoes and mosaics, like those found on the early Christian basilicas in Rome and Ravenna. Alberti subsequently published the architect's theoretical rationale for the design of the church; as a result, there is hardly a single larger fresco cycle dating from the 15th century to be found in Florence.

Lorenzo Ghiberti (1378–1455)

Lorenzo Ghiberti—goldsmith, sculptor, and art theoretician—operated one of the most important of the Florentine art workshops, from which a number of noted artists including Michelozzo, Uccello, and Pollaiulo emerged. In many respects, Ghiberti was a rival of Brunelleschi's, and conflict became inevitable after they were both commissioned with the construction of the cathedral dome. Certainly the vague intuitions that constituted Ghiberti's contribution to the project, as well as his jealous intriguing, must have brought the reserved Renaissance architect Brunelleschi to the brink of despair.

In contrast, the merit of Ghiberti's masterwork, the doors of the baptisterium in Florence, is uncontested. According to Vasari, even Michelangelo extoled their perfection: "They are so beautiful that they could probably stand at the gates of paradise"—but this proves to be a thoroughly ambiguous remark, for a baptisterium, as the place where pure and innocent children are christened, is in itself an image of paradise.

One of the three bronze doors had already been completed by the sculptor Andrea Pisano (1290/95–1348/49); now, following a long period of catastrophes in Florence—bankruptcy, bad harvests, plague, and famine—the city had finally taken up the project again.

left:
Filippo Brunelleschi, *The Sacrifice of Isaac*, 1401–1402. Bronze, 20¾ x 16½ inches (53.3 x 42 cm). Museo Nazionale del Bargello, Florence.

right:
Lorenzo Ghiberti, *The Sacrifice of Isaac*, 1401–1402. Bronze, 20¾ x 16½ inches (53.3 x 42 cm). Museo Nazionale del Bargello, Florence.

In 1401 a competition was announced for the design of the two other complementary doors of the baptistry. Both Brunelleschi and Ghiberti, as well as many other sculptors, submitted entries. Such open contests, which anyone could enter, were a custom peculiar to Florence. They not only fostered competitive thinking but also democratized the evaluation of art. Furthermore, since the maintainance of artworks and churches in any case resided in the hands of the guilds, the democratization of art in Florence was quite advanced.

Jacopo della Quercia (1374–1438), *The Sacrifice of Isaac*, ca. 1430. Marble, 37½ x 34 inches (96 x 87 cm). Porta Magna, San Petronio, Bologna. Jacopo della Quercia also took part in the competition for the doors of the baptistery. The composition of his surviving bas-relief of *The Sacrifice of Isaac* monumentalizes the elements of the story by reducing the content to its rudiments. The artist placed his focus on the human figure and its expressiveness, and for their sake rejected decorative details.

Brunelleschi's and Ghiberti's relief models for the baptistery doors have survived. Both artists treated the theme of Abraham's willingness to sacrifice his son, Isaac, but the artists' expressions of the theme are completely different. Both works include the sacrificial alter, two servants, a donkey, a goat, an angel, and Abraham himself, who is about to cut Isaac's throat. Of the two designs, Ghiberti's is doubtless more elegant and clearly presented. The development moves from left to right: The servants and the donkey stand outside the range of vision behind a rock; Isaac has cast off his clothes and kneels tied to the wood of the sacrificial fire; Abraham is poised in the act of striking him. Just at this moment, the angel of the Lord appears and commands Abraham to offer a ram, which has entangled itself by its horns in a bush, in place of his son—everything portrayed exactly as it is narrated in the Bible.

In Brunelleschi's version, Abraham's left arm occludes the act of the sacrifice itself; the main interest of the relief seems instead to reside in the donkey and the two servants sitting in front of the altar, who are straining to avoid awareness of the horror going on immediately behind them. Beneath the altar, the fire has already been lighted that will be used to sacrifice the ram, which is scratching its head as it waits.

Lorenzo Ghiberti, *Cain and Abel*, relief from the *Door of Paradise*. Gilded bronze, 34 x 34 inches (87 x 87 cm). Baptistery, Florence. According to St. Augustine, Cain and Abel represent the divine economy, with pure faith (Abel) and the error of heresy (Cain). The relief on the *Door of Paradise* is the second of ten; the scenes accrue additively and do not make any convincing attempt at central perspective.

For Brunelleschi, it is not the *storia,* or unfolding of the events, that stands in the foreground of his portrayal of Abraham and Isaac, but the joy pervades his presentation of nature and antiquity. The figure of the ram scratching its head, already employed by Nicola Pisano (see p. 29), is in fact borrowed from antiquity, as is the variation on the famed removal of the thorn by the servant portrayed on the left.

A 34-member jury declared Ghiberti the winner. Between 1403 and 1425, he produced the first door with scenes from the New Testament. With 28 small panels set into quatrefoils, Ghiberti's work formally recalls the first pair of doors by Andrea Pisano; after the completion of Ghiberti's work, however, Pisano's door was unceremoniously removed from the main portal to a side entrance.

During the more than 20 years of work on the door, Ghiberti's status as a sculptor had undergone a fundamental change. Through his artistic success, above all in his activity on the construction of the cathedral, he had achieved a position that raised him above the artisans who were carrying out his designs. Now, in the creation of the last door, not only was he able to leave behind the the constricting and stylistically worn out quatrefoil design, but he reduced the number of reliefs to ten: "I was granted the freedom to carry them out in the manner I believed the most perfect, most decorative, and most rich." Even if this freedom referred only to the formal design and not to the content of the relief, it was completely unprecedented in the social history of art.

Each panel of the baptistery door now contained a complete story told in up to six scenes. The square picture fields are bounded by molding containing recesses and frames surrounding statues of the prophets and sybils, busts (including a self-portrait; see illustration p. 16), and a heretofore unequaled variety of detailed plants and animals. This, the most modern work of its day, earned the position of honor on the building: Ghiberti's second portal, the *Gate of Paradise*, was installed in the central position on the east, facing the cathedral—a place originally intended for Christian subject matter drawn from the New Testament, for Christ stood for the rising son, the resurrection, the new life. The *calimala*, the powerful guild of merchants who tended the baptistery and had granted Ghiberti the commission, was by now so convinced of his artistic excellence that it was even able to set aesthetic considerations above religious ones—an act that seems to have become conceivable only in the 15th century.

Lorenzo Ghiberti, *The Story of Joseph*, Relief on the *Door of Paradise*. Gilded bronze, 34 x 34 inches (87 x 87 cm). Baptistery, Florence.
The six panels of the *Door of Paradise* present such a sophisticated and interwoven series of scenes that it is impossible to interpret them without knowledge of the story. In addition, with his depiction of a circular building, Ghiberti offers a comment on contemporary architecture.

In the course of work on the final portal door, there seems to have been a clear change in Ghiberti's understanding of art. The clarity of the *storia* gives way more and more to *varietas,* or a multiplicity of figures, postures, and architectural images from various points of view. The illusion of reality increasingly pierces through the biblical message, in spite of the repeated official texts of the church opposing this development: Pictures were supposed to instruct the illiterate members of the congregation as clearly and understandably as possible, to hold the deeds of Christ and the saints continually before the eyes of believers, and to evoke emotions that would lead to piety.

Donatello (Donato di Niccolò di Betto Bardi, 1386–1466)

The most important artists of the early Renaissance not only worked in the same city, but also contributed to the same building, the cathedral of Florence. Within what was geographically an extremely confined area,

Donatello, *David*, 1408. Marble, height 74½ inches (191 cm). Museo Nazionale del Bargello, Florence.

Nanni di Banco, *Isaiah*, 1408. Marble, height 75¼ inches (193 cm). Cathedral, Florence.

the new style unfolded into a broad spectrum of possibilities involving, as the competition between Ghiberti and Brunelleschi had already demonstrated, all available artistic media.

Donatello clearly stood on Brunelleschi's side of the Renaissance. Whereas the International Gothic style is still evident in the fine-boned elegance of Ghiberti, Donatello's figures reveal an increased individuality and a greater plasticity clearly derived from the artist's intensive study of antiquity and human anatomy.

As decoration for the tips of the buttress, the organization of cathedral masons planned to set twelve marble prophets. In 1408, they commissioned Donatello and his elder colleague, Nanni di Banco (1373–1421), to create statues of *David* and *Isaiah*. The drapery of the robes is malleable, and the figures stand in the classical posture of counterpose. *Isaiah*'s head and his naked arms refer back to ancient sculpture, whereas the tender, soft facial expression of Donatello's *David*, with his almond-shaped eyes, corresponds to the Florentine ideal of beauty of the Trecento. This *David* was erected in the Palazzo Vecchio and, like Michelangelo's *David* almost a hundred years later, became a symbol of the city of Florence, which extoled David above all as the victor over formidable enemies, both without and within the city walls.

For one of the niches in the campanile of the cathedral, Donatello created between 1423 and 1426 the sculpture known as the *Zuccone* (pumpkin)—a bald-headed figure supposedly representing the prophet Habakkuk. Without giving the sculpture any specific attributes that would identify the model, Donatello had created a type whose strikingly individual physiognomy was unlike anything made up to that time in Italy. The great fall of the *Zuccone*'s heavy robes underscores the corporality of the prophet, who looks down upon the observer from his elevated niche.

Another milestone in the history of European art is the childlike bronze *David* that Donatello cast as a life-size freestanding statue, thus freeing sculpture from the clutch of architecture, which had for centuries chiefly employed it merely as a decorative element. For the first time since antiquity, a nude now stood as a fully autonomous figure, and one that was finished in the round. These sculptures broke new ground, fulfilling criteria that came to be accepted as a matter of course a century later by sculptors such as Benvenuto Cellini, who argued that "[A]mong all the graphic arts, sculpture is seven times greater [than the others]; for a statue to be a sculpture, it must have eight sides, and all must be equally good."

Donatello, *Habakkuk*, 1423–1426. Marble, height 76 inches (195 cm). Museo dell'Opera del Duomo, Florence.

In Donatello's *David,* the boy's shoes and shepherds' hat emphasize his nakedness. With the oversized sword of Goliath in his hand, David has cut off his opponent's head, on which he now smilingly sets his foot in a posture of victory. The naturalness of the figure, as well as the naturalistic, erotic shaping of details—such as the folds of skin around the neck and armpits, and the long feather on Goliath's helmet that reaches up David's inner thigh—led Vasari later to exclaim, "This figure contains so much of nature, life, and softness, that [contemporary] artists thought it must have been cast around a living figure."

Donatello, *David,* ca. 1445. Bronze, height 61½ inches (158 cm). Museo Nazionale del Bargello, Florence.

Donatello was also the leading master in the development of a new and dramatic style of relief that paired a great plasticity of foreground with an almost engraved, flat background (*rilievo schiacciato*). More than any other artist, Donatello stamped the character of early Renaissance sculpture in Italy and also carried the ideals of Florentine art into the north, in particular to Padua, where he created an altar in the Cathedral of the Holy Antonius, and an equestrian statue, the *Gattamelata*. His influence extended far into the 16th century, still finding expression in the work of artists such as Cellini and Michelangelo.

Masaccio (Tommaso di Giovanni di Simone Guidi, 1401–1428)

The work that decisively established the artistic fame of this painter, who died at the age of 27, is his fresco of

Masaccio, *Trinity*,
ca. 1427. Fresco, 260 x
123½ inches (667 x 317
cm). Santa Maria
Novella, Florence.
In particular, the archi-
tecture of the fresco, the
first precisely reckoned
example of central per-
spective in the Renais-
sance, caught the atten-
tion of later art historians and challenged
them to attempt to
reconstruct the pictorial
space.

the *Trinity* in Santa Maria Novella in Florence. The representation of the six figures at the foot of the cross is not the painting's chief claim to fame, however. On the lowest step, still outside the painted chapel, kneel the patron and his wife at prayer; above them are Mary and St. John standing on either side of the crucified Christ, who is supported by God the Father. The appearance of the painted figures is at once simple and statuesque. The coloration is economically executed in alternating reds and blues. Only in the clothing of God the Father do both colors appear together, for God unites all opposites. Because Mary and John are clearly smaller than the other four figures, the figures do not help establish spatial depth in the paint-ing; instead they remain resolutely in a flat triangular composition.

In contrast to the figures, it is the painting's architectural depth that gives it historical significance. Masaccio's fresco survives as the first picture in which Brunelleschi's concept of central perspective is perfectly applied; it is even possible that Brunelleschi himself had a hand in the design of the painting. The picture has inspired much still unsettled debate about how exactly the spectator is supposed to understand the floor plan and elevation of the architecture in spite of—or because of—the precise construction of the three-dimensional space. Critics have even gone so far as to attack the postures and sizes of the figures because they did not conform to various art historians' understanding of the construc-tion of spatial depth. In fact, it must be admitted at the start that it is not really possible to establish the actual framework of the room with absolute certainty.

A theory on the spatial construction of the *Trinity* fresco

Underlying the picture is the idea of humans as the measure of all things, a notion the Renaissance adopted from antiquity. Here, man is literally reduced to his basic framework, which provides the unit of measurement for the painting: The skeleton depicted in the fresco's base measures precisely 65¾ inches (167 cm). The distance between the pillars framing the painting are in a 1:1 relation to the figure, the height of the arch in a 2:1 relation, and the total height of the painting in a 4:1 relation.

The vanishing point of the painting is the sill on which the patrons are kneeling. Because the figure of God the Father is standing on a raised sill against the back wall of the room and at the same time supports the cross, the space depicted in the painting cannot in reality be very deep. The "room" takes on the character of a niche.

The recessed rectangular ceiling panels are portrayed from a strongly inferior perspective. Thus the theoretic standing point of the observer, which determines the spatial illusion, lies quite close in front of the painting, at a distance of about 11 feet (3.5 m), or twice the length of the human unit of measurement. If one assumes the vanishing point lies equally far behind the surface of the painting, then the depth of the wall niche is in a 2:1 relation to its width, and if the crossbeams of the crucifix correspond to Vitruvius's sense of human proportion, then the cross is exactly in the middle of the room.

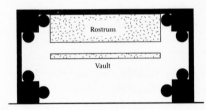

In exemplary fashion, Masaccio's fresco bids farewell to the intuitive grasp of space, and proposes an alternative aesthetic based on numbers and simple, harmonious proportions. At the same time, the artist integrates the monolithic grieving figures and faith into the painting to create a memorial built of deep sincerity.

The frescoes of the Branacci Chapel, begun by Masaccio and Masolino and completed by Filippino Lippi, became a pilgrim's shrine for Renaissance artists. There, for the first time, they could see their painting ideals made manifest. The painter Tommaso de Crisoforo Fini, known as Masolino da Panicale (1383–1447), worked together with Masaccio. Because of the difference in their ages, the elder Masolino has often been assumed to be the teacher of the younger artist. In fact, however, the artistic innovations in their work stemmed beyond a doubt from Masaccio. In the *Healing of the Lame* and the *Resurrection of Tabitha*, on the other hand, we see a work that stemmed almost wholly from Masolino, who combined two scenes in a single fresco. On the left, St. Peter is healing a lame man, of whom the *Acts of the Apostles* reports (3: 1–2):

Masolino and Masaccio, *Healing of the Lame* and the *Resurrection of Tabitha*, 1425. Fresco, 96½ x 229⅛ inches (247 x 588 cm). Cappella Brancacci, Santa Maria del Carmine, Florenz.

"Now Peter and John going up to the temple at the hour of prayer, the ninth hour. And a man lame from birth was being carried, whom they laid daily at that gate of the temple which is called Beautiful to ask alms of those who entered the temple." The beggar is depicted foreshortened from the back, as was traditional in presentations of this episode, and the style of the temple architecture also corresponds to the prevailing imagination of the day. Peter and John step up to the beggar, and the bearded apostle reaches a summoning hand toward him to command, "In the name of Jesus Christ of Nazareth, walk" (Acts 3:6).

The beggar has apparently not yet understood that he is about to embark on a new life in which he will walk about and jump and praise God (see Acts, 3:8), for his hand motion seems more as if it is awaiting a charitable pittance rather than a miracle. The story could not be presented more economically in its composition and details, more sympathetically, and at the same time more consistently with the biblical text.

Almost the mirror image of the first scene is portrayed in the *Resurrection of Tabitha*, which depicts the resurrection of a noble and generous woman whose story is also told in the *Acts of the Apostles*. Peter, this time accompanied by two men who had summoned him out of the neighboring town, commands the dead woman, who was known as "Gazelle," to rise up. "And she opened her eyes, and when she saw Peter she sat up" (Acts, 9:40).

In the Renaissance architecture that forms the backdrop of the picture, several typical Renaissance figures have entered, seemingly unaffected by holy events. The two young men who have inserted themselves between the scenes, seemingly in order to present the latest autumnal fashions of 1425, provide the picture with an actual contemporary reference; their vain costumes furthermore offer a grotesque contrast to the earnestness of the event, as if, in the words of Roberto Longhi, they are emerging from "the oppressive atmosphere of an eventless late afternoon" reflected in the everyday ordinariness of the vignette in the background.

For the great art historian Longhi, the Brancacci Chapel offers an inviting opportunity to characterize a "soft heart toward a neo-Giottesque return;" while in contrast, he finds that Masaccio is "a consummate genius" who must again and again intervene in order to save his colleague's perspectival construction and the harmony of the scenes in the last minute. Thus the stage setting that forms the background for the *Healing of the Lame* and the *Resurrection of Tabitha* comes, according to Longhi, from Masaccio, while the foreground was painted by Masolino. "Whoever cannot grasp this contradiction, however ... may wave goodbye to all hope of grasping even an inkling of the art of perspective."

It has always been the practice of art history to create heroes, to set individual artists on a pedestal and honor them, and thus to satisfy a desire for a glamorous star-cult. But the glorification of artistic heroes requires the levying of merciless criticism against everything that might spread the odium of mediocrity and backwardness. This practice has never occurred more clearly or in a smaller space than here. The Branacci Chapel is a unique total work of art, but it is also a flagrant example of the tendency of art history to construct myths: Masolino becomes the hopelessly outdated Gothic; Masaccio, in contrast, the modern savior, the genius who dies young.

Masaccio, *The Banishment of Adam and Eve* from the *Garden of Paradise*, ca. 1425–1427. Fresco, 80 x 35 inches (205 x 90 cm). Cappella Brancacci, Santa Maria del Carmine, Florence.
The individuality of the figures, the immediacy of the action, and the perspectival construction made Masaccio's work into an object of study for subsequent generations of artists.

Developments in the North

Claus Slater

1348
Founding of the
University of Prague
1350
The *Legenda aurea* is
published in a German
translation
1367
The Fugger family comes
to Augsburg as weavers
ca. 1370
Beginning of the Cologne
school of painting
1386
Founding of the oldest
German university at
Heidelberg
1388
Founding of the
University of Cologne
1429
Charles VII crowned king
of France
1441
Nicolas of Cusa, German
philosopher and bishop,
attempts to re-establish
papal rights in Germany
and to reform the clergy;
Portugal begins slave
trading
ca. 1445
Gutenberg invents the
printing press with move-
able type
1453
End of the Hundred
Years' War

Claus Sluter, *Moses
Fountain* (detail), 1395.
Stone, figures ca. 70
inches (180 cm) high.
Chartreuse de Champ-
mol, Dijon.
At the Burgundian court,
artists began creating
works in the new spirit
of the Renaissance at
about the same time as
the Italian masters.

The court of Burgundy

Parallel to the developments in Italy, the late 14th century also witnessed the transformation of the court of
Burgundy into a forum where the International Style
and the French knightly culture joined to produce a late
golden age. In 1363, Philip the Bold, youngest son of
King John II of France, had received Burgundy as a
dukedom, and his successors, John the Fearless and
Philip the Good, succeeded in expanding the area of
their hegemony considerably. Flanders was annexed as
early as 1384, leading to an intensive artistic exchange
between the two lands. Situated between Germany and
France, Burgundy became an important power and the
fulcrum of artistic development north of the Alps for
the next century.

Claus Sluter (1355/60–1405)

In the work of Claus Sluter (1355/60–1405), who was
summoned by Philip the Bold from his native Holland
to the Burgundy court at Dijon in 1385, the study of
human anatomy opened the way to a naturalism that
must have shocked his contemporaries. In daring "an
amazingly bold grasp of reality" (A. Schmarsow),
Sluter is a unique and towering phenomenon of the
early Renaissance. His work spans the gap between the
so-called "soft style"" of the International Gothic and
the development of individualized character types.

Until this point, such
individualized "types"
were unimaginable
north of the Alps, and
even in Italy such figures
were not seen, other than in
early experiments, until
they became dominant in
the following century. By the
time Donatello's early *David*
was commissioned by the
city of Florence (see
illustration on p. 48),

Sluter's career had already ended. His fame was established by his *Fountain of Moses* in Dijon, with its six large, precisely detailed figures of the prophets. Sluter's artistry made a lasting impression on subsequent French artists of the Renaissance.

Robert Campin (pre-1380–1444)

Likewise, the influence of the Netherlander Robert Campin on the following generation can hardly be overestimated. Campin's love of detail, meticulous use of color, and naturalism had an enduring effect. And yet, as late as 1900, Campin was still fully unknown: Not a single work had been attributed to him. His name arose occasionally only in connection with Rogier van der Weyden; Campin, a master from the little town of Tournai where his workshop became a center of northern panel painting, was mentioned in a document as Rogier's teacher. Today, however, there is widespread agreement that the works of the so-called master of Flémalle are also by Campin. Thus, from what was once an anonymous figure arises one of the leading artists of his age, next to Jan van Eyck.

Robert Campin (Master of Flémalle), *Annunciation*, Mérode Altar (center panel), ca. 1425. Oil on wood, 24½ x 24½ inches (63 x 62 cm). Metropolitan Museum of Art, New York. The art of depicting supernatural events within a bourgeois ambiance, and giving them material reality through a malleable treatment of space, distinguishes Robert Campin and makes him, along with van Eyck, a founder of the Old Netherlandish school of panel painting.

When the Burgundy court migrated from Dijon to Bruges and Lille after the English victory at the battle of Agincourt in 1415, the influence of the Netherlandish painters grew, and they could now cultivate their talents in their own homeland.

Jan van Eyck (1390–1441)

Jan van Eyck was not only a court painter for Phillip the Good, but also traveled as a diplomat to Spain and Portugal. After 1430, he lived chiefly in Bruges, where

Jan van Eyck, *The Marriage of Giovanni Arnolfini*, 1434. Oil on wood, 32 x 23¼ inches (81.8 x 59.7 cm). National Gallery, London. The stage-like setting of the ideal bourgeois world is complete down to the smallest detail. The convex mirror, hanging in a central position, reveals the room and the couple from behind, as well as the painter at work, who immortalized himself in an inscription on the wall: "johannes de eyck was here. 1434." The convex reflection of the wealthy merchant's world is surrounded by scenes from the Passion of Christ. To the left hangs a rosary, to the right a broom, completing the bourgeois world with the self-sacrificing passion of the marriage between faith (rosary) and domestic order (broom).

he functioned as both a court painter and as the official painter for the city. Van Eyck became famous for his detailed naturalism, his determined use of oil paint (Vasari even asserted that van Eyck was the inventor of this new medium), and his deceptively realistic treatment of surfaces. In place of the fine-limbed figures, ornamental architecture, and tower-filled landscapes created by painters such as Melchior Broederlam, for example, a generation earlier at the Burgundy court, van Eyck substituted naturalism, spatial realism, and panoramic landscapes, thus creating a new kind of illusionistic pictoral unity.

Decisively at odds with Italian representational art, however, is the northern acceptance of the often chaotic assumptions in both the natural and the human environments. Netherlandish artists lavished their fascinated attention on the wealth of details in a scene drawn directly from life, which, although artificially arranged, was at all times oriented on reality. The appearance of the objects themselves was the decisive criterion, in contrast to the Italian emphasis on formal geometric construction, to which naturalistic details were merely fitted and subordinated. Such "Vitruvian" ideals, however, had no impact on Netherlandish painting. The notion, prevalent in the Italian Renaissance, that objects could be formed more perfectly by art than by nature would have struck the Netherlanders as absurd.

The *Marriage of Giovanni Arnolfini and Giovanna Cenami* captures the union of the scions of two Italian merchant families. Both came originally from Lucca but had spent most of their lives in the north, where they became quite rich, as is apparent in van Eyck's double portrait. The pair hold hands between the window opening onto the world and the enormous marriage bed. In front of them, the little dog stands for faithfulness, and above hangs a chandelier in which a single candle—signifying the first glow of new life?—is burning. The bride also has gathered her gown into a shape that suggests pregnancy (which, however, was destined never to occur in this marriage).

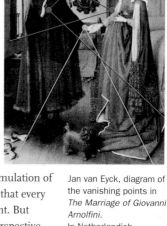

Jan van Eyck, diagram of the vanishing points in *The Marriage of Giovanni Arnolfini*.
In Netherlandish painting, the treatment of space tends to be based on optical perception and effect; spatial construction derived from central perspective remains of secondary importance.

The idealized room that van Eyck seems to have recreated with such amazing verisimilitude is, on closer inspection, in fact a symbolically loaded arena—a well-balanced artistic composition in which every free area of surface is filled up with shoes, exotic fruits, noble candelabras, and an Anatolian rug. The scene is in fact an accumulation of stage props—and so it is hardly surprising that every part of the room has its own vanishing point. But because the paths of the various lines of perspective running between window and bed are softened by overlapping (the vanishing point of the window lies to the right, that of the bed to the left), the room appears larger than its actual narrowness suggests. The expanding effect of the multiple vanishing points on the distance from the ceiling to the floor is, on the other hand, responsible for the extraordinary depth conveyed by the picture.

Rogier van der Weyden (ca. 1399–1464)

After his apprenticeship with Campin, Rogier van der Weyden became not only the master of the sculptors' guild in Tournai (1432), but also the official city painter of Brussels. In addition, he was the father of a painting dynasty that survived for four generation. His sons Jan and Peter, his grandson Goossen, and his great-grandson Rogier II made the name van Weyden known throughout civilized Europe, occasioning even the Italian critic Vasari to admit that the *pater familias* "painted very beautifully in oil." The philosopher and theologian Nicolas of Cusa, who had studied law in

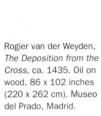

Rogier van der Weyden, *The Deposition from the Cross*, ca. 1435. Oil on wood, 86 x 102 inches (220 x 262 cm). Museo del Prado, Madrid.

Heidelberg and Padua and took part in the Council of Basel in 1432, called van der Weyden the greatest of painters, and Bianca Maria Sforza, Duchess of Milan, sent her court painter Zanetto Bugatto (d. 1476) to van der Weyden in Brussels to acquire the latest painterly refinements. The two artists, however, were soon at loggerheads, with the Netherlander declaring that he would admit Bugatto back into his workshop only if the Italian would swear to abstain from wine for a year. If one may surmise that behind this dispute deeper differences of outlook were at work, then the argument may also be interpreted as a symbol of the opposing understandings of art north and south of the Alps. Italian tendencies in general made their way into the north only slowly and, whereas van der Weyden became one of the most influential painters in Netherlandish and German art, the diligent Bugatto has been almost totally forgotten.

Van der Weyden's *Deposition from the Cross* serves as a contribution in the longstanding argument over which is the higher art—painting or sculpture? This battle between the artistic paragons had already spawned a series of excited literary commentaries in Italy (see page 49), but the Netherlands were more reticent with statements of theory. The *Deposition*, however, achieves a sculptural character through its emphasis on linear rhythms and its refusal to play with the effects of spatial depth. The painted figures are embedded in neither an architectural structure nor a landscape, but seem, rather, to compose a golden shrine of figures, such as a sculptor might well have chosen for his theme. Instead of creating the character types usually found in wood carvings, however, van der Weyden develops a subtly colored and intimately emotional interlacing of figures with which he casts the arguments of the sculptors' guild well into the shadows.

Panel painting held the position of the noblest of the graphic arts; panel painters tended to be prosperous and, through their guilds, controlled the admission of new colleagues, who had to present both examples of their work and a sum of money before they were allowed to work. (Painters on canvas, on the other hand, commanded as yet much less respect, and for a long time labored chiefly on temporary decorations for feasts and ornamental pictures.) It seems that a number of masters of the time wanted to prove that good painting was the equal of sculpture. Jan van Eyck and Hugo van der Goes (ca. 1440–1482), for example, imitated sculpture with *grisaille*, or gray-on-gray, painting on the daily, or exterior, side of their altars; when the

Hugo van der Goes, Portinari Triptych (exterior, left), ca. 1475/76. Oil on wood, 98½ x 55 inches (253 x 141 cm). Galleria degli Uffizi, Florence.

Hugo van der Goes, *Adoration of the Shepherds*, Portinari Altarpiece (middle panel), ca. 1475/76. Tempera and oil on panel, 98½ x 118½ inches (253 x 304 cm). Galleria degli Uffizi, Florence.
This tryptich immortalized the arts patron Tommaso Portinari, an agent for the Medici Bank in Bruges, along with his family.

wing panels were opened on feast days, however, the full glorious color of the painting shone forth.

The merchant Tommaso Portinari, who had led the trading office of the Medicis in Bruges for 15 years, commissioneed the most monumental altar of the old Netherlandish tradition for the church of Santa Maria Novella in his native city of Florence—a painting that proved to have a lasting influence on the generation of artists around the time of Ghirlandaio and Botticelli. The figures of the altarpiece, set in a barren and frosty winter landscape, are clearly earthly and true to nature. At the same time, the altar is enriched with icono-graphic references and symbols. The harp above the portal of the stone house in the middle panel refers to King David, from whose family Jesus was to come, according to prophecy; the vases placed so prominently in the foreground contain irises, a fire lily, and a columbine with seven blossoms—all reference to the purity and sufferings of Mary and the sacrificial death of Christ. The grain indicates the place of the event, Bethlehem, literally the "house of bread."

Lucas Moser, *Sea Jour-ney,* Magdalen Altar (left panel), 1432. Mixed media on wood, 117 x 93½ inches (300 x 240 cm). Parish church, Tiefenbronn.

Lucas Moser (ca. 1390–after 1434)

In Germany, as in Italy and Burgundy, noteworthy artistic centers began to arise. Not only in the flourish-ing merchant centers of Nuremberg, Frankfurt, and Cologne, but also in the provinces, there appeared extraordinary signs of a new age in art.

In 1648, the archives of the free imperial city of Weil (in southern Germany) were destroyed, making re-seach on the painter Lucas Moser almost impossible. All that is known about him derives from an odd verse he inscribed on one of the most splendid altars of all time, the *Magdalen Altar in Tiefenbronn:* "Cry, art, cry, and complain sore;/ no one values you any more. alas. 1432. lucas moser. painter of wil [*sic*]. master of this work. pray to god for him."

The painting discloses the date, name, and origin of the artist—but what else does the inscription mean? Does it bespeak the suffering of a misunderstood avant-garde artist, or the farewell of an aging one going to his rest? Even if Moser originally came from the rather provincial region around Tiefenbronn, it seems unlikely that he spent his entire life there. His pictures, with their finely differentiated details, have the effect of miniatures and are reminiscent of the Burgundian tradition. Also, the oak panels on which they are painted were rarely used in southern Germany—but are typical of Robert Campin and Stefan Lochner in the north.

The altar at Tiefenbronn depicts three episodes in the life of St. Mary Magdalene—her journey by sea, her arrival in Marseille, and her last taking of the bread of communion—all are united across the three panels by a shared landscape and gothic architecture. The source of the story is once again the beloved collection of saints' legends, the *Legende aurea*, according to which, after the death of Christ, his enemies attempted to get rid of his disciples, including Mary Magdalene, and set them adrift in a boat. "But through the grace of God, it so happened that they landed in Massilia. There they found no one who would take them in, and so they remained under the porch canopy of the pagan temple.... Then, after some days, Magdalene appeared to the wife of the prince in a dream and said: 'Why do you let the holy ones of God suffer hunger and cold, when you yourself sit here in great wealth?'"

In the painting, all is minutely and magnificently represented in a unified and realistic atmosphere full late Gothic joy in ornamentation. In *Sea Journey*, Moser experimented with a subtle play in the gold background. The golden sea leads directly across the golden halo into the delicate mountain landscape in the distance, beyond which a flat golden heaven is disclosed. The right panel narrates the last station in the life of Magdalene, her death after taking final communion: "On this day, around this very hour, Maximinus went forth alone to church as he was commanded. There he saw Mary Magdalene in the angels' choir, for they had led her there. She was lifted two ells above the earth, and stood in the midst of them."

Modern Gerthener, *The Worship of the Three Kings*, Tympanon, ca. 1425. Liebfrauenkirche, Frankfurt am Main. Each of the kings, preceded by a herald with a flag, comes to worship from a different direction. In the foreground they display their gifts.

Modern Gerthener (pre-1370–1430)

That artists north of the Alps had to contend with problems of social acceptance no less than their colleagues to the south is clear from the example of the Frankfurt architect and sculptor Modern Gerthener, who remained inscribed in official documents as a "stone mason," and later still as "workman."

Gerthener was among the well-to-do citizens of Frankfurt; in fact, he became its mayor. In this office, he expanded the city's fortifications, bridges, and towers. As church architect, he erected the transept and tower of the large Frankfurt parish church (erroneously referred to as a cathedral). Gerthener's reputation spread far beyond the city, to the point that he was called in as a consultant on the building plans for the tower of the Strasbourg minster.

It was challenge enough to be responsible for the imposing building projects of an ambitious free imperial city, where the German kings had been elected since 1356 and home to the largest market and fairgrounds of Europe. But Gerthener also attempted to maintain his position as a leading sculptor, as is evident in the *Trinity Tympanon* in the Church of Our Lady. The richly costumed troops of the three holy kings, who are recognizable by their flags, approach from three directions and meet in front of the stall at Bethlehem. Three angels are singing, the oxen and donkeys gaze on, and in the distance, over mountains rising in ranges above each other, fat sheep are grazing. The work thus unites the layered pictorial construcion familiar since Pisano—although it now conveys a far greater depth of scene—together with figures painted in the "soft style" that is perfectly suited to the theme of the picture. This combination of elements opens a path from the Late Gothic to a new, more workable pictorial conception.

Stefan Lochner (ca. 1410–1451) and Konrad Witz (ca. 1400–ca. 1445)

The most important painting master in Cologne in the first half of the 15th century was Stefan Lochner. Born in the far south of Germany, in Meersburg on Lake Constance, he made his mark on the art of the city of Cologne, which, ever since its acquisition of the relics of the three holy kings in 1164, had continued to grow into a center of worship of the three saints. Even the banishment of the archbishop by the patricians and citizens in 1288 did nothing to diminish the status of the city as a pilgrims' destination.

Lochner's *Mother of God in the Rose Arbor* is probably his last work. The pictorial theme of Mary in the Garden of Paradise probably origi- nated in upper Italy, and, like Stefan Lochner himself, made its way down the Rhine to Cologne.

The intimate devotional picture painted on an oak panel depicts an angel-ringed Madonna seated on a garden bench under a canopy of leaves. The blood-red roses are refer- ences to both the love and the death of Christ, while the white lilies symbolize the pure virginity of Mary, and the apple refers to the victory over the guilt incurred by the first human parents. The natural details are

Stefan Lochner, *Mother of God in the Rose Arbor*, ca. 1450. Mixed media on wood, 19½ x 15½ inches (50.5 x 40 cm). Wallraf-Richartz Museum, Cologne. The engraved gold background emphasizes that the scene does not belong to earthly regions, but is set in the Garden of Paradise. Two angels appear to be pulling back the curtains to allow us a momentary glimpse into the heavenly spheres.

worked into an elegant and idealized setting. Once again, it is clear that in the art of all northern European artists of the 15th century, the characteristics of the International Gothic style are still influential.

Even after the Great Schism, when year-long debates in the reform councils—first in Pisa (1409) and Constance (1414–1418), and later in Ferrara (1438–1439), Basel (1431–1439), and Rome (1512–1517)—had achieved only very doubtful success in efforts to strengthen and unify the Church, every council nonetheless provided a multicultural gathering that undoubtedly had an inspirational effect on the artists of the time. Like Lochner, his long-forgotten south-German colleague Konrad Witz was also affected by this spirit.

Konrad Witz, *Saint Christophorus*, ca. 1435. Oil on wood, 39½ x 31½ inches (101 x 81 cm). Öffentliche Kunstsammlung, Basel.

Until late into the 19th century, the works of Master Konrad were variously attributed to Guido da Siena (early 13th century), numbered generally among the "French-Burgundian School," or compared with those of Gerrit von St. Jans (late 15th century)—all surmises that lead one on a careening tour through entirely different lands and epochs. Finally, the stylistic similarities between the mysterious works and a St. Peter's altar in Geneva signed by a Magister Conradus of Basel suddenly defined an *oeuvre* that could be identified with a definite person, even if the details of that artist's life must remain a matter of conjecture. All that is known for certain is that Witz was a member of the painters' guild in Basel in 1434, and that he must have been acquainted with the art of van Eyck and Campin. Witz was the first German artist to place his figures in a three-dimensional space and who strove to reproduce the texture of cloth realistically.

In considering northern European art history—as with that of some of the Italian cities—one occasionally receives the impression of a very closely intertwined development. Perhaps this is because far fewer names are known in the north than in Italy, and as a result, one succumbs to the temptation of establishing connections between the few individual artists about whom something is known. Thus, Sluter is said to have influenced Campin, who, under his "provisional" name of the Master of Flémalle, was for a long time thought to have been a pupil of van Eyck's. But, it turns out, Sluter was in fact the teacher of Rogier van der Weyden, who in turn influenced the art of Lochner, among others. Moser's work was not determined by Campin and Lochner; Lochner's style is related to that of Konrad Witz, who in turn owed a great deal to van Eyck, and so on *ad infinitum*.

We know that Albrecht Dürer studied the works of his predecessors minutely during his travels, and the contacts among artists may have been similarly close among the contemporaries of van Eyck, one possible point of intersection being, of course, the Burgundian court. In the end, who was influenced by whom, or where and how the contacts were established, remain questions without any clear basis for answers. The Early Renaissance in the north remains an equation with many unknowns.

Exchange with Italy

In 1453, Constantinople was conquered by the Turks; before the end of the year, a group of important Greek scholars emigrated to Italy. Although most of the foreign artists were musicians, there also were a considerable number of graphic artists who felt drawn to the rich cultural landscape of Italy. Some, such as Juraj Dalmatinac and Ivan Duknovic, came from Dalmatia; others, like the icon painter Janos Platypodis and Markos Cauzo, originated in Crete. The majority of immigrants, however, came from the north, including Joos van Gent at the court of Urbino, or Petrus Christus in Milan. The life and the social acceptance of artists differed greatly north and south of the mountains. As late as 1494, when Dürer arrived in

Joos van Gent, *The Communion of the Apostles*, 1473–1474. Oil on wood, 110½ x 118½ inches (283 x 304 cm). Palazzo Ducale, Urbino.

Venice, he wrote to his friend Pirckheimer, "Here I am a gentleman, at home, a sponger."

It is significant that after a milestone of the Renaissance such as Jan van Eyck's altar in Ghent, little further development occurred in the field of painting. Not until the 1560s did new tendencies become evident in the work of Hugo van der Goes and Joos van Gent (J. v. Wassenhove, ca. 1435–after 1480).

The painter Joos, or Jodocus, was inducted into the sculptors' guild of the city of Ghent as master. He enters the historical records again as surety for Hugo van der Goes (1465), and then, after taking out a loan for a journey to Italy, departs, leaving the home field free for his colleagues. In 1473 he surfaces in Urbino as Giusto da Guanto, or sometimes Giusto di Alemagna ("Justus the German"; to the Italians, the difference between the Netherlands and German territory was not very important). In Urbino, he made a considerable contribution to the decoration of the ducal palace. One of the panels he painted seems originally to have been intended for Piero della Francesca to carry out. The Italian artist had been in Urbino as early as 1469 as a guest of Giovanni Santi to take a look at the wooden panel; but apparently, Joos van Gent was either deemed an equally good alternative, an acceptable second choice, or possibly even recognized as a master to whom one could give preference. With his precise, fine oil technique, he made friends for himself not only in Urbino, where he collaborated on the furnishing of the *studiolo*, or contemplation and reading room, of Federico da Montefeltro, but also in Rome. Much more observant than Rogier van der Weyden, for example, who had also traveled to the Eternal City in the jubilee year 1450, Joos came to terms with Italian art. Rogier van der Weyden, in contrast, had only once allowed himself to be carried away from his trusted northern preference for detail when he expressed admiration for an artist like Gentile da Fabriano (see p. 39). "Rogier imported Netherlandish art; Joos transplanted it." (Friedlander)

The lack of enthusiasm displayed by many northern artists toward Italian art was returned with interest: Northern European painting found even less favor among the Italians. Although a number of individual artists had made the trek from the Netherlands to Italy, where they were warmly received, or their works had become known through the agency of Italian trade outposts, such as that of the Medici in Bruges, northern art tended in general to be greatly misunderstood. Michelangelo spoke for many of his colleagues in excoriation: "Flemish painting ... will generally speaking please the pious better than any Italian work, which can never move one to tears; while the Flemish works call up many tears... It will please the women, especially the very old and the very young, and the monks and nuns and certain nobles as well who have no feeling for harmony. In Flanders they paint with the intention of deceiving sensory perception.... And, even if it pleases some, all this is accomplished without logic or artistic ability, without symmetry or proportion, without skill, taste, or audacity, and above all without significant content and vitality."

Here we learn, as is usual in such declarations, more about the speaker than about the subject. We can hear

Antonello da Messina,
St. Hieronymus,
ca. 1455. Oil on wood,
17¾ x 14 inches (45.7 x
36.2 cm). National
Gallery, London.

Michelangelo's contempt for tasteless clergy and sentimental women, and discern his own artistic maxims: symmetry, proportion, and audacity. The depiction of reality with the sole ostensible intention of deceiving the eye and the alleged lack of content in Netherlandish art contains the same fundamental misunderstanding reiterated by Roberto Longhi in 1914: "In no Italian artist will you find anything even remotely approaching objectivity in the rendering of reality. And I would like to add at the same time: That is fortunate! Respect the earnestness of these [northern] artisans who devoted themselves heart and soul to the simple assumption that life contains enough significance to be painted with color and brush—without reflecting that replication is always superfluous—these artisans, through their attention to color and brush, forget that it is absolutely necessary for art itself to be life, and that it therefore must lead a separate, independent life that it determines for itself. Only Italian art understood this truth, and thus without exception all European styles of art, at least in the area of painting, originally emanated from Italy."

For a thoroughly Italian master like Michelangelo, the rejection of the rational ideal, the wealth of detail, and the misapplied materiality of northern European art was incomprehensible. Some Italian artists, however, took another approach. Antonello da Messina (ca. 1430–1479), for example, became acquainted with the art of the north entirely in the south, and according to legend, is responsible for popularizing oil painting in Italy. He was of Sicilian origin and worked in Messina and Naples. There he came into contact with the Flemish-Burgundian style that originally had reached the Naples area through the Anjous, who had defeated the ruling Staufers at the behest of the pope in 1266–68, and later through Alfons of Aragon, who had in turn replaced the last of the Angevins in 1442.

Antonello carried these important impressions with him to Venice, where his painting of St. Hieronymus stands out for its fascinating wealth of detail, and seems moreover to have been drawn directly from contemporary life. The saint is not depicted as an emaciated aesthete, but as a well-nourished monk at work in his orderly *studiolo*. He has furthermore carefully removed his slippers before stepping into the study chamber. In the background, a lion roams through the wide Gothic arch in which the saint's study is set. There is a disturbing spaciousness about the architectural props that makes the scene look like a carefully composed stage set viewed through a stone proscenium arch.

The *Studiolo*

The connection between the *vita activa* and the *vita contemplativa* was one of the fundamental themes of the Renaissance. For example, as a soldier, Federico da Monte-feltro was more inclined toward the active side of existence, but the rounded formation of a person required precisely an intellectual development, symbolized in arrangements for an undisturbed place of retreat in the ducal palace. "The need to learn and develop oneself privately formed the basic requirement for a space that would allow undisturbed reading and writing. Until into the 12th century, such a claim existed almost exclusively for only a single caste of society: clerics and monks." (W. Liebenwein). The hermetic character of the *studiolo* (also called *scrittoio*) had its roots in the strict periods of study required in the daily routines of the Carthusians, Cluniacs, Cistercians, and other monastic orders.

In secular Renaissance study chambers, or studies, which were an integral component of palace design from the second half of the 15th century onward, the traditions of the antique world naturally also played a role, whether for Humanists such as Niccolò Niccoli and Poggio Bracciolini, or despots like Leonello d'Este and Cosimo de' Medici. The new palace of the Medici family in Florence (see p. 110) harbored several *studioli* in the various apartments of the palace.

In windowless chambers decorated with illusionistic intarsia designs, one could pursue one's studies in the ducal palace in Urbino under the eyes of the portraits of intellectual greats, and periodically enjoy a break on the loggia, which offered a broad view of the surrounding landscape. Nothing served better to demonstrate learning than the library of a prince; and thus a swarm of scribes were constantly engaged in copying the works that were then shown to educated or powerful guests.

Jan van Eyck, *Ghent Altar* (exterior),
completed 1432. Oil on wood, each panel
ca. 146¼ x 50¾ inches (375 x 130 cm).
St. Bavo, Ghent.

The long history of political and
military conflict between Flanders
and Burgundy—in which Ghent had
often played an important role—had
no effect on Jan van Eyck's
relationship with his patrons, city
councilman Jodocus Vijd and his
wife Elisabeth Borluut, or with
Philip the Good, duke of Burgundy.
The duke unquestionably attended
the unveiling of this most splendid
altarpiece of early Netherlandish
painting as a matter of course.

After its completion in 1432, the
Ghent Altar was often subjected to
the vicissitudes of fate during the
following centuries. To preserve the
altar from the outbreaks of iconoclasm growing out of the Reformation, the altar was removed from the
church and hidden in the city hall.
During the French Revolution,
Napoleon's troops claimed the altar
as war booty and carried it away to
France. Only in 1816, after
Napoleon's defeat in the Battle of
Waterloo, was the altar restored to
Ghent. But even greater dangers
lurked at home, when the panels
were dismantled and sold piecemeal
by a vicar general. Elements of the
altar later turned up in Brussels and
Berlin. After the First World War,
the altar was once more removed to
France, only to be carried off by
Hitler to Neuschwanstein. As it
became apparent that Germany
would be defeated, the altar was
deposited in an Austrian salt mine
for safekeeping. Finally the altar was
returned to Belgium once again by
the Allies after 1945.

As a football in world history, the
altar was damaged several times and
has therefore undergone a number
of restorations (one might even call
them renovations).

In the history of art, the altar has
always been an incunabulum. As
such, it has always been accorded
respect, even though enthusiasm for
the picture itself waned through a
number of centuries, its artist fell
into relative oblivion, and the sparse
historical facts about the painting
became overshadowed by legends.

The inscription of the altar gives
the date of its completion, names
the patrons, and identifies the brothers Hubert and Jan van Eyck as

artists. And now one of the great games in art history begins: Which artist is responsible for which portion of the picture? Because the paint was applied in many layers, one may surmise that the two artists did not work side-by-side; rather, it is likely that one painted over the work of the other—a hypothesis supported by the painting's stylistic consistency. Historically, the inscription has seemed to offer precious little help in distinguishing between Jan and Hubert: "[PICTOR] [H]UBERTUS [E] EYCK. MAIOR QUO NEMO REPERTUS / INCEPIT PONDUSQ[UE] IOHANNES ARTE SECUNDUS / [FRATER PERFUNCTUS] IUDOCI VIJD PRECE FRETUS / VERSU SEXTA MAI COLLOCAT ACTA TUERI." (Square brackets designate interpolations.) Translated, the inscription then reads: "The painter Hubert van Eyck—greater than he could not be found—began this work. His brother Jan, second in art, completed the work at the wish of Jodocus Vijd. With this verse, he invites you to view on May 6 what has been created."

In presenting himself in a secondary position, whether Jan van Eyck was deferring to his brother—who had died in 1426—or expressing his true evaluation of himself, is not at issue here. Art history, in any case, does not share his judgment. Interestingly, another way of reading the inscription has been proposed: If one assumes FICTOR (sculptor) as the first word instead of PICTOR, and if one reads PICTOR PERFECTUS in place of FRATER PERFUNCTUS, then the phrase ARTE SECUNDUS may mean "in art the second chronologically." The inscription, reconstructed by Lotte Brand Philip, would then read: "The sculptor Hubert van Eyck... began the work, and Jan, the excellent painter, in art chronologically the second, invites you...."

It is possible that Hubert had no part in the painting itself, but carved a magnificent frame that has since been lost. There are clearly occasions when inscriptions hide as much as they reveal.

However one reads the text, the celebration on May 6, 1432, marks a milestone in European art history. Nor, apparently, did the painting tarnish the reputation of the patron: Jodocus Vijd became mayor of Ghent the following year.

Jan van Eyck, *Worship of the Lamb*, Ghent Altar (interior). Oil on wood, 52½ X 91½ inches (135 x 235 cm). St. Bavo, Ghent.

1452
Frederick II crowned Emperor of the Holy Roman Empire in Rome

1453
Constantinople conquered by the Turks; end of the Eastern Roman Empire

1458
Ferdinand I becomes King of Naples; Matthias I Corvinus becomes King of Hungary

1459
Cosimo de' Medici establishes the *Accademia Platonica* (school for translation of Platonic texts) in Florence

1463
François Villon, vagabond French poet, reprieved from gallows, is sentenced to 10 years' exile

1498
Savonarola is hanged and burned as a heretic

The inventors of the new style

The innovations of the four outstanding figures who are generally accounted as the "inventors" of the new style of the early Italian Renaissance—Brunelleschi, Ghiberti, Donatello, and Masaccio—landed on fertile ground. Their ideas were immediately taken up by their contemporaries and then adopted by their successors, who proceeded to vary and develop them. In particular, the new interest in perspective and in the realistic representation of nature invited much experimentation. Later, important inventions, such as the printing press and oil painting, made their way into Italy in the course of the 15th century and also came to have a lasting effect on art south of the Alps.

"O what a charming thing is perspective"

After the death of his father in Pisa, Antonio Pisano (ca. 1395–1455), known as Pisanello, moved with his mother from his home city to Verona. By 1415, when he was 20, he apparently obtained a position for himself as an artist, for he began work on the fresco cycle left unfinished by Gentile da Fabriano. Like Gentile,

Pisano's career was marked by many moves from one court to another within Italy. He served as a court artist in Mantua but was also active at the palace of the Visconti in Pavia, and worked on the Lateran Palace in Rome and at the court of Alfonso of Aragon in Naples as well. No other artist of the early Renaissance mastered the precise art of the nature study better then Pisano. In short, he made a name for himself as a universal artist and entered the annals of art history as a painter and graphic artist, sculptor and architect.

Pisanello, *St. George and the Princess* (detail), 1436–1438. Fresco, 87 x 242 inches (223 x 620 cm). Santa Anastasia, Verona.

Perhaps most important historically were Pisano's medallions, which he adorned with individualized profiles of the various princes of the land. These profiles not only gratified the immediate vanity of the princes, but also paved the way for the later development of portraiture in Italy.

Like Pisano, Paolo di Dono (ca. 1397–1475) was a contemporary of Masaccio. His favorite theme was animals, especially birds—an emphasis which supposedly earned him a name in history: *Uccello* (bird).

According to Vasari, Uccello had another passion even greater than his interest in painting birds: Uccello "would have been the most charming and rare spirit of all the artists blossoming in the wake of Giotto if he had invested as much diligence in painting men and animals as he spent time and effort in painting objects in perspective.... These pieces are indeed beautiful and appeal to the senses, but whoever devotes too much of himself to such things throws away his time and exhausts his talent by overloading his understanding with difficulties that often cause a fresh and fruitful spirit to become dry and heavy." Vasari was writing, however, from the standpoint of a man of the 16th century to whom all the tricks of perspective were already familiar. For him, the techniques of perspective were necessary but not very interesting artists' tools. Uccello was in fact one of the pioneers of the art of illusion, and spent entire nights working on his studies. When his wife attempted to talk him into finally going to bed, he supposedly murmured in answer, "O what a charming thing is perspective!"

Pisanello, *Leonello d'Este*, medallion, front side, 1441–1442. Bronze, 4 inches (10.3 cm). National Gallery of Art, Washington D.C. Such coins and medallions had a long history in the dissemination of the image of the prince of the land. The striking profile view at once maintained a sense of proper distance and recalled ancient traditions.

1469
Isabella of Castile marries Ferdinand of Aragon; Lorenzo de' Medici holds power in Florence
1484
Papal bull of Innocent III instigates widespread persecution of witches
1494
King Charles VII invades Italy

Antonio del Pollaiuolo (ca. 1432–1498), *Profile of a Young Woman*, ca. 1465. Tempera on wood, 20¼ x 13½ inches (52 x 35 cm). Gemäldegalerie, Berlin. The aristocratic tradition of the unapproachable profile made its way into painting.

73

Like most artists of his time, Uccello based his nature studies on medieval theories. Mountains arose as a result of subterranean wind or fires, hills through a blistering of the earth, and cleft rocks through stone made brittle by fire. In painting mountains, many artists apparently used the technique of *ex minimo*. As described by Cennini, students were required to use a broken piece of rock as a model for entire mountains in their paintings. Uccello's *Saint George* includes just such hollowed-out mountains. Not until the 15th century did artists realize that such "air bubble theorems" (A. Perrig) had no place in the precise study of nature for which they were striving. The hollow-mountain theory was geologically untenable—and was incapable of answering the vexing question of the origins of rivers that poured down from the mountains.

Paolo Uccello, *St. George and the Dragon*, ca. 1456. Tempera on canvas, 22¼ x 29 inches (57 x 74 cm). National Gallery, London.

The equestrian statue as Renaissance monument

In 1436, Uccello painted a memorial to the Condottiere John Hawkwood (d. 1398) for the Florentine cathedral. The fresco depicts Hawkwood—known to the Italians as Giovanni Acuto for his 20 years of service at the head of the mercenary army hired by Florence—as a mounted knight. Viewed from a strongly undershot perspective, the sarcophagus that serves as a socle for the bronze monument rises on consoles. The horse and rider, however, are painted as if at the viewer's eye-level, thus creating a contradiction that seems inconsistent with that fanatic of perspective, Uccello. Perhaps the painter was ordered to temper his extreme perspective—just as he had been forced by the commissioners of the Opera del Duomo to destroy his first draft because the work supposedly "was not painted as it should be."

Close upon the heels of Uccello's fresco of the mounted knight, with its roots so obviously in antique tradition, followed real monuments in bronze. During the whole of the Middle Ages, the antique equestian memorial to Marcus Aurelius had stood for all to admire in front of the church of St. John Lateran. (Only in 1536 did Pope Paul III move it to the Capitol.) In 1436 Donatello erected for the Republic of Venice the first modern equivalent of the Aurelius monument in the square before the Church of St. Anthony: A memorial to the rather unsuccessful, but faithful *condottiere* Erasmo Narni, known to history as *Gattamelata* (honey-sweet cat).

Andrea di Cione (1435–1488), known as *Verrocchio* (true eye), inherited Donatello's throne both as a sculptor in Florence and in service to the Republic of Venice. No lesser artists than Ghirlandaio, Leonardo da Vinci, Lorenzo de Credi, and Pietro Vannucci Perugino came to study at Verrocchio's influential workshop, which was the second largest in Florence after that of Antonio de Pollaiuolo. For Venice, which had itself produced only a few great sculptors, Verrocchio created the *Statue of General Colleoni*. The dynamism of the horse and brutal expression of the rider personified the essence of the military quest for power and easily overshadowed the more static works of Uccello and Donatello.

To the Renaissance public, the equestrian statue embodied a combination of physical strength and spirit— a unity of swift action and intellectual discipline—the very virtues that characterized a ruler. At the same time, for the Renaissance artist, the figure of the mounted knight opened the door to the possibilites of monumental free standing work, such as had constituted sculpture's highest task in the ancient tradition.

Paolo Uccello, *Equestian Statue of Giovanni Acuto* (detail), 1436. Fresco transferred to canvas, 285½ x 157½ inches (732 x 404 cm). Santa Maria del Fiore, Florence.

Andrea del Verrocchio, *Equestrian Statue of Bartolomeo Colleoni,* 1481–1488/96. Gilded bronze on marble socle, height of statue 13 feet (4 m). Campo SS. Giovanni e Paolo, Venice. In his arrogance, the equally rich and feared Condottiere Colleoni provided in his will that Venice would inherit his wealth if he were allowed to build himself a monument in front of San Marco. The Venetians found a loophole to outsmart him—they erected the monument in front of a school named San Marco, instead of the famed church.

Between faith and politics—Fra Angelico (ca. 1387–1455)

The first surviving painting of the Dominican monk Fra Angelico dates from the year 1433—apparently, he began his career as a painter at an advanced age. His two masterworks, the frescoes in the monastery of *San Marco* in Florence (after 1436) and in the chapel of Nicolas V (after 1446) display a serene maturity that essentially excludes the possibility of further development. In the painting of the 41 cells at San Marco, Fra Angelico probably had an entire troop of assistants at his disposal. In Rome, his worth in relation to his fellow artists is clearly visible in the payroll lists of the Vatican: Jacomo da Poli and Giovanni della Checha received 12 florins per annum, Benozzo Gozzoli 84, and Fra Angelico 200.

As has so often been the case, Vasari's estimation has been a major determinant of the image of this artist, also. Humble, unassuming as a man, talented and religious in his painting—these are the qualities long associated with Fra Angelico, the "last bloom of the Middle Ages" (F. Schottmüller). The organization of the painted figures in the monks' cells at San Marco is clear and understandable; the colors are largely reduced to the primaries, especially in the passion of Christ. The paintings make no effort at dramatic narrative, but seem instead to call forth worship and contemplation. They are filled with details from daily life and citations from contemporrary architecture, but nonetheless remain in the tradition of restrained Gothic elegance.

The image of the introverted, backward-looking monk Fra Angelico turning away from the base world in order to devote himself to his sacred art is probably inaccurate in spite of the religiosity of

Fra Angelico, *Annunciation*, ca. 1449. Fresco, 84½ x 125 inches (216 x 321 cm). San Marco, Florence.

his themes. This religious element so characteristic of his paintings was in fact an element of daily politics. From 1419, Florence was the seat of the church council that had begun in Basel and was continued in Ferrara. In Florence, the most important clerics of both the Western and Eastern churches met together and set the tone of events. In 1434, Cosimo de' Medici returned to Florence from his family's first exile and commissioned Fra Angelico with the decoration of the monastery in which a cell was to be prepared as a retreat for Cosimo himself. In the same year the pope-in-exile, Eugene IV, also returned to Florence and set himself up in the Dominican monastery of San Maria Novella. The power and influence of the Dominicans cannot be overstated, and Fra Angelico, who had been a vicar at the convent of Fiesole by Florence since 1432 and afterward stepped into the shoes of St. Anthony himself as prior, was much more of a public figure than his meditational pictures suggest.

Fra Angelico, *Mocking of Christ*, 1440. Fresco, 73⅓ x 67 inches (188 x 164 cm). San Marco, Florence.
The *Mocking* reduces Christ's tormenters to surreally moving arms and a head hanging in space. The Redeemer, enthroned on a podium, is at once ruler of the world and helpless victim. But the humiliation legitimates the limitless claim to power of the Messias. At his feet, Mary and St. Dominic sit in a posture of reflection and seem to invite the observer to follow their example.

Filippo Lippi (1406–1469)

One of the most important painters of the early Florentine Renaissance is Filippo Lippi, who first lived as a monk in the monastery of St. Maria del Carmine before he became acquainted with the qualities of a more worldly life. Monastic self-indulgence was of course nothing new to the age, but the behavior of the 50-year-old Lippi, who fled the monastery together with the young nun who had sat as model for a portrait of the Madonna, was scandalous for even those times. But neither this, nor his falsification of documents, nor breaches of contract dented his popularity as a painter.

In the church of his monastery he had been able to follow at first hand the creation of Masaccio's masterpiece, the frescoes in the Branacci Chapel—a work that the friar's son was eventually to complete. From Masaccio's painting, Lippi drew his fluid corporality

Filippo Lippi, *Holy Virgin with the Child Jesus and Angels,* ca. 1464. Tempera on wood, 37 x 24 inches (95 x 62 cm). Galleria degli Uffizi, Florence.

and meticulous perspective; from his residence in the Carmelite cloister in Siena in 1428, his figures acquired their soft courtly grace; and a sojourn to Padua advanced his sense of color.

The Medici on pilgrimage to the Holy Land: Benozzo Gozzoli's glorification of his patrons

At the same time that Fra Angelico was passing the torch to his pupil Benozzo Gozzoli (1420–1497), the Medici also underwent a generational change. With the new generation, the simplicty and clarity of the frescoes in the monastery of San Marco gave way to opulence. The modesty of the first powerful members of the Medici family—which was to rule the city of Florence almost without interruption for nearly 300 years, until 1737 when the family finally died out—ended soon and abruptly with Piero and especially Lorenzo, whose epithet "il Magnifico" was well-earned. His impressive new palace, built on the main thoroughfare between the cathedral and San Marco, was completed under the direction of Cosimo de' Medici; afterwards, Piero negotiated with the painter Gozzoli for the decoration of the family chapel.

With its tapestry-like character, Gozzoli's fresco *The Procession of the Three Holy Kings* discloses the sojourn of the kings and their trains with unrestrained splendor. The patrons also appear in the procession, just as earlier members of the Strozzi family had been included in the panel painting of Gentile da Fabriano (illustration p. 39). Now, however, with the Medici, the patrons were no longer included merely as attendants; they were portrayed as the holy kings themselves. At the head of the train rides a youthful Lorenzo, the reins of his white horse adorned with the Medici coat of arms; in his wake follow Piero and Cosimo.

The motif of three generations of Medici on their way to the Holy Land—placed as it was in a family chapel that served simultaneously as an audience chamber for guests and envoys—amounted to an unmistakeable political declaration concerning the church's power and its military intentions in the East. Only six years before the fresco was begun, Byzantium had succumbed to the onslaught of the Ottomans and the Hagia Sophia, one of the most venerable buildings of Christendom, had been converted into a mosque. The pope felt it incumbent upon himself to encourage Christian princes to take up arms against the heathen tide. Pope Nicolas V and his two successors, Calistus III and Pius II, called for a crusade, this time not for the reconquest of the holy shrines of Christendom, but to build a bulwark against the advances of the Turks.

An ambitious ruling family—one, moreover, with designs of its own eventually to set one of its own members on the lucrative pontifical seat—could not in principle appear to ignore such a call to arms. In reality, however, the military blow to the Christian world had quite clearly been greeted by the Medicis with something less than dismay. At the height of their personal power and prestige in Europe, any such call to engagement stemming from merely moral or religious conviction could only be perceived by the Medicis as a burdensome interruption of their own plans.

In the great Medici design, artists, too, had become an integral component of the accumulation of family power and magnificence. Artists' services were employed not only for the obvious glorification of the ruling family, but also in a kind of cultural diplomacy. From the 1480s onward, Lorenzo il Magnifico

Benozzo Gozzoli, *The Procession of the Three Holy Kings* (detail), 1459–1461. Fresco, width ca. 24½ feet (750 cm). Palazzo Medici-Riccardi, Florence.

consciously fostered the dissemination of Florentine artists among the courts of Italy in order to help himself establish and maintain contact with the leading families of Italy.

The inevitable counterreaction to this tactic and its prestige-oriented political timbre was not long in coming. Lorenzo's actions not only forced the end of Florence's role as leader in the realm of the arts, but also contributed to a political about-face in Italy. After his death in 1492, his son Pietro the Unlucky was exiled for a number of years while the monk Savonarola took over the governance of the city. Suddenly, at the intellectual center of the Renaissance a local reform movement was set in motion that, on the one hand, castigated the worldliness of the Vatican, but did not go so far as to question the dogmas of the popes, as Martin Luther would soon do in northern Europe. As an apocalyptic visionary, Savonarola preached abstinence, faith, and the renunciation of worldly display. With his rigorous program he soon found himself in opposition to the Roman church, which brought about his downfall and execution.

Piero della Francesca, *The Meeting of the Queen of Sheba and Solomon* (detail from the *Legend of the Holy Cross*), ca. 1460. Fresco, 131 x 291 inches (336 x 747 cm). San Francesco, Arezzo.

Urbino and Piero della Francesca (ca. 1420–1492)

The princely portrait in full profile, already known from Pisanello's coins and medallions, became popular among the ruling houses throughout central Italy in the mid-15th century. The sharp lines of such a profile portrait lent the face a striking and distant expression, which emphasized the dignity of the subject. Inaccessible and classic in posture, but courtly and naturalistic in expression, the profile portrait seemed an ideal blend of Renaissance ideals.

Probably the most famous double portrait of the Renaissance is that of the *Condottiere Federico da Montefeltro* (1420–1482) and his wife Battista Sforza (d. 1472). Despite his irascible temperament, Federico, Duke of Urbino, was undoubtedly the most accessible of the neighbors of the Medici in Florence. With the rough-hewn Castruccio Castracane holding court in

Piero della Francesca, *Double Portrait of Battista Sforza und Federico da Montefeltro*, ca. 1472. Oil on wood, each panel 18⅓ x 13 inches (47 x 33 cm). Galleria degli Uffizi, Florence.

The profile view selected by the artist offered his subjects precisely the image they desired, for the right half of Federico da Montefeltro's face had been disfigured in a tounament mishap. In the painting, the only visible reminder of the accident is the duke's strikingly hooked nose—an unmistakable hallmark of the duke. Piero della Francesca probably used a death mask as model for the profile of the duke, Battista Sforza, who was a noted patroness of the arts. After nine births, she died of exhaustion after finally producing a son.

Lucca, the Medici had their hands full—just as they did with the elegant and well-educated tyrant Sigismondo Malatesta in Rimini, against whom Pope Pius poured out his scorn: "It has gone so far that he even does violence to his daughters and sons-in-law. As a youth, he already was chasing after the women and enjoyed corrupt indecencies. He often abused young men. For the sacrament of marriage he had no respect…. He has outdone every barbarian in cruelty. With his bloodied hands he martyred the guilty and innocent alike."

In comparison to such a scoundrel, Federico seemed, of course, a cavalier. For his court, he erected the most imposing palace of his day and immediately signified his wish to develop it into an important forum for Humanism and the arts. After a stormy period of transition (see p. 112) beginning with the murder of his half-brother Oddantonio by his own retainers and an attempted putsch against Federico himself, the duke opened his court to such masters as Joos van Ghent and Pietro Berruguete and thus fostered the interchange between the cultures north and south of the Alps.

In his youth, Federico had lived and studied for two years with his relatives in Mantua. As an illegitimate offshoot of the Montefeltro family, he now used the arts to legitimize his claim to power, to demonstrate his successes, and to advance his daughters and his son into the great families of Italy. His strategic

Piero della Francesca, *Flagellation of Christ*, ca. 1458. Tempera on wood, 22¾ x 31¾ inches (58.4 x 81.5 cm). Galleria Nazionale, Urbino.

marriage politics brought union with the Colonna, Malatesta, Gonzaga, and della Rovere families. Federico's grandson, Francesco Maria Della Rovere (1490–1538), eventually ascended to power in Urbino. Meanwhile, Cesare Borgia, by far the most feared incarnation of willful power and violence in Italy, had appropriated Urbino and a great part of central Italy for himself. After the death of his father Pope Alexander VI, Julius II—who was born a della Rovere—forced Cesare back to his old boundaries as the new pope undertook efforts to refortify the church as a whole.

Piero della Francesca can be seen as the first artist outside of Florence who was able to provide impetus to the further development of the early Renaissance. Born in the tiny city of Borgo San Sepulcro, he became the most important painter of Umbria. As an apprentice to Domenico Veneziano, however, he also lived a number of years in Venice. There he had been inspired by the atmosphere of Humanism, as well as by Uccello's studies in perspective and the frescoes of Masaccio, before creating his trailblazing fresco cycle *The Legend of the Holy Cross* (1452–1466; illustration p. 80) for the Bacci family and his panel paintings for the Duke of Urbino.

For Piero, depth of field and fluidity of figure are not ends in themselves, as they sometimes seem to be in Uccello. Rather, they are at the service of his themes. His subtly colored, seemingly archaic figures inhabit a

Flagellation of Christ by Piero della Francesca

The Flagellation of Christ is one of the most discussed paintings in the history of Italian art. Except for the identity of the painter, everything about the picture has come under violent discussion—even the dating and the patron, as well as the subject itself. As already seen with *The Ghent Altar* by van Eyck, every attempt at solution raises new and complex questions. Agreement, however, can be quickly established for the left side of the picture: It obviously depicts the scourging of Christ. That this scene, taking place in the background of a carefully worked-out Renaissance hall, is the actual theme of the painting, however, is questionable because of the three figures in the right foreground. The two halves are not only spatially separated, but—as already noted in an inventory of 1744—also temporally separated from one another. This oldest source on the picture claims the three men represent the dukes Oddantonio, Federico, and Guid' Ubaldo Montefeltro of Urbino. But Federico is nowhere to be seen, so art historians soon rejected this interpretation. Every alternative suggestion fundamentally alters the meaning of the picture. Following is a brief selection of interpretations as compiled by Carlo Ginsburg:

1. The three men are simply passersby. (C. Gilbert)
2. The bearded figure is Judas, who is being paid his silver by the members of the Sanhedrin. (E.H. Gombrich)
3. As in traditional iconograpy found in old painting, the three figures witness and discuss the scourging. (C. Gilbert)
4. The men are Sanhedrin members who do not wish to be sullied before the Passover (see John, 18, 28). (L. Borgo)
5. The picture was occasioned by the call of Pius II in Mantua to the princes to participate in a crusade. (Clark)
6. The young man is Federico's half-brother Oddantonio, together with his two bad counselors, with whom he was murdered in 1444. (R. Longhi)
7. The man in the brocade robe is the clergyman of the papal treasury, Giovanni Bacci; opposite him is the bearded Greek prelate Bessarion, who was visiting Rome in 1459; between them stands the bastard son of Federico, Buonconte, who was declared by his father to be legitimate, but died at age 17 in 1458. (C. Ginzburg.)

If one accepts thesis 2, the picture is without contemporary reference—but the silver coins that should be central to the theme of a painting with a purely religious reference are noticeably absent. Thesis 5 equates the act of the scourging with the captivity of the church, which must be freed by the initiative of the popes (see Gozzoli, p. 78.) According to thesis 6, the young tyrant becomes the victim of his advisors, who are mirrored in the soldiers whipping Christ. Thesis 7 is a form of condolence message: Bacci and Bessarion, both friends of the talented and highly educated young man—who is moreover depicted as pale and remote in time through his antique clothing—sent the panel to the grieving father Federico in Urbino.

The variety of interpretations seems to be endless, but the mystery of the unusual composition on two spatial and temporal planes still remains. *The Flagellation of Christ* is a good example of how mosaic stones of small, hard facts can be freely augmented by the ideas of art historians into full and fascinating explanations.

timeless present. Reduced to clear primary forms and arranged according to mathematical principles, they caught the attention of artists and art historians of the classical modern school who rediscovered Piero della Franceso with enthusiasm for the 20th century. Closer inspection, however, reveals coded political messages hidden behind the artist's seemingly naive presentation of Christian iconography. This profane core, such as one commonly find in the works of other artists of the period, takes a particularly refined form in Piero: It reflects a pragmatic approach to religion as an instrument of power in the hands of church leaders and princes.

Pietro Perugino, *Christ Giving the Keys of the Kingdom to St. Peter*, 1480–1482. Fresco, 132½ x 214½ inches (340 x 550 cm). Sistine Chapel, Vatican, Rome. A grid seems to determine the painting, which is clearly divided into fore-, middle-, and background with its symmetrical architecture. Above the central event of the picture rises an octagonal church in the form of a paragon of centralized construction dreamed of by architectural theorists.

Perugino (Pietro di Cristoforo Vannucci, 1445/48–1523)

The history of the different Italian cities followed an extremely varied course during the Renaissance, depending heavily upon the practices and excesses of the given ruling families. In Mantua, ruled for three hundred years by the Gonzaga family, or in Ferrara, where the ancient and noble Este clan (forefathers of the German Welfs) held sway, the environment was comparatively civilized and tranquil. In cities like Perugia or Orvieto, in contrast, family feuds set the tone of the political climate. In a half-century, Orvieto was plundered eight times, and in Perugia, the family quarrel between the Baglioni and the Oddi constantly claimed new victims.

From the midst of these bloody conflicts emerged the "angelic" and "sweet" works of Perugino, as described by one of the scouts of Lodovico il Moro (see p. 86). In his art, Perugino created a primarily religious and harmonious antithesis to Peruria, addressing the fundamental readiness of its storm-tossed citizens for remorse and penance. The occasion of a new murder always called for elaborate ceremonies of remorse, prayers, ritual cleansings, and sermons from Fra Bernardino da Siena on the transitory nature of all earthly things—until the whole cycle began over again.

By 1520, feuds had brought the city to the point of exhaustion, reflected in the stiff formal elegance and fatigue of Perugino's style during these years. His creative high point had already been reached in the last two decades of the 15th century. For the Sistine Chapel he had painted a series of frescoes, including a *Giving of the Keys* that depicted highly respected biblical figures with unusual clarity in an idealized Renaissance plaza. The fresco demonstrates Perugino's mastery of the techniques of perspective and composition of figures within a carefully ordered spatial field.

Michelangelo had little use for the art of Perugino—perhaps in part because Perugino was the teacher of his arch-rival Raphael—and apparently made no objection when the frescoes of his older colleague were destroyed to make room for his own *Last Judgment*.

The popes' lack of artistic understanding and respect had a long tradition, according to Vasari. Cosimo Rosselli (1439–1507), "who felt himself to be weak in invention and drawing, tried to hide his mistakes by painting with the finest possible ultramarine blue, as well as many other lively colors, and a good deal of gold." Although Rosselli could not escape the ridicule of his peers, Pope Sixtus IV readily declared his works the most successful. Work on the chapel concluded in 1482, but Perugino, Ghirlandaio, and Botticelli had apparently already vacated Rome, incensed at the pope not so much for his flawed taste as for his failure to pay their salaries.

Sandro Botticelli, The Birth of Venus, *ca.* 1485. Tempera on canvas, 67 x 108½ inches (172 x 278 cm). Uffizi Gallery, Florence.

Far more often than in previous centuries, Renaissance princes sent agents out into the world to investigate the quality of artwork and the personalities of artists in other regions of Italy. Lodovico il Moro, Duke of Milan, ordered such a report in 1490 before engaging painters for the decoration of the *Certosa* in Pavia.

These artistic agents gathered information about the competence of panel and fresco painters, as well as about the current state of competition among the artists, who often worked together on a single project, such as the Florentine cathedral. For example, "Sandro Botticelli: An excellent painter on both wooden panels and the walls. His works convey a manly impression (*aria virile*) and are completed with the highest degree of understanding (*optima ragione*) and perfect proportion (*integra proportione*). Filippino, the son of the very good painter, Fra Filippo Lippi: A student of the previously mentioned Botticelli and the son of the most unique artist of his times. His works possess a sweetness (*aria piu dolce*), but, I believe, are not very artistic. Perugino: An original master, especially on walls; his works have something of the angelic about them (*aria angelica*) and are very sweetly executed *(molto dolce)*. Domenico Ghirlandaio: A fine master on the wooden panel, and still better on the wall; his works make a good appearance (*bona aria*). He is an experienced man who can accomplish a great deal of work. All these painters, with the exception of Filippino, have already proved

Filippino Lippi, *Martyrdom of St. John the Evangelist*, 1497–1500. Fresco. Cappella Strozzi, Santa Maria Novella, Florence.

Pietro Perugino, *Apollo and Marsyas*, ca. 1490. Tempera on wood, 15¼ x 11⅖ inches (39 x 29 cm). Louvre, Paris.

themselves in the chapel of Pope Sixtus IV. Later, they all worked in the Spedaletto of Lorenzo il Magnifico (these works are now lost), and it is really a good question, to whom the palm of victory belongs."

Evaluating the works of these masters today inevitably raises the question of how our viewpoint has changed over the centuries. We can understand a number of the agent's references, the "angelic" elegance of Perugino's figures, for example, or the "perfect proportions" of a Botticelli. But what might "manly appearance" and "highest understanding" mean when applied to the same artist? Furthermore, do the proportions of a Botticelli really differ so greatly from those of his fellow artists? And how can it be that a painter whose works possess

"sweetness," but nonetheless are "not very artful" is even seriously included for consideration along with the others?

Apparently, the significance of the agents' words and the weighting of criteria during the Renaissance were quite different from our modern understanding—a fact one must constantly keep in mind when reading contemporary historical sources.

We will never know to what extent the Duke of Milan understood his agent. What is certain is that the duke commissioned altar paintings from Perugino, Raphael's teacher, and the "unartful" Filippino Lippi. The oversight of the project, however, was awarded to the Piedmontese artist Bergognone (1453–1523).

Domenico Ghirlandaio, *The Confirmation of the Order of St. Francis by Pope Honorius III*, 1482–1486, Fresco, Holy Trinity, Florence.
The Italian art historian Roberto Longhi warns us of Ghirlandaio's "frivolousness, his brazen joy in production, and his realism." In emulation of Masaccio, he enriched his works in the northern tradition by providing small, anecdotal details, as well as with excellent portraits. Ghirlandaio mastered scenes with masses of figures by means of his clear organization and finely-tuned colors, but nonetheless preferred to confine the scenes within "fresco cages."

Sandro Botticelli (Alessandro di Mariano Filipepi, 1445–1510)

Sandro Botticelli experienced a personal renaissance in 19th-century England. Alerted by the writings of Alexis-François Rios, the Pre-Raphaelites (including Dante Gabriel Rossetti and Sir Edward Coleyn Burne-Jones) discovered an idol in the Italian master. They used the elegiac and heathen elements they believed they found in his work to justify their own decadence.

Sandro Botticelli, *Primavera (Spring)*, ca. 1482. Tempera on wood, 79 x 122½ inches (203 x 314 cm). Galleria degli Uffizi, Florence. Botticelli endowed his classical beauties with a particular sensuality. His love of lively mythological scenes combines with luminous coloration to give his paintings the character of opulent festivals.

Botticelli, a native Florentine, worked for a number of influential families in his city. For the Medicis, he carried out a commission for a (probably posthumous) portrait of Giuliano Medici, who had been assassinated in a plot by the Pazzi family. Upon his return from the Sistine Chapel, where he had worked with some of the greatest masters of his time, Botticelli undertook his most important and most mysterious works, the *Birth of Venus* and *Spring*. The latter is probably an allegorical illustration of fertility and rebirth, as signified in the blossoming of the springtime. In the midst of a flowery meadow within an orange orchard stands a madonna-like Venus (goddess of love) and the youthful Mercury with sword and winged sandals. He parts the clouds with his herald's staff, while between him and Venus the Three Graces are dancing while a blind Cupid shoots them with his arrow and the deities of spring enter the scene from the right.

Mantua and Andrea Mantegna (1431–1506)

The great painter and antique collector Andrea Mantegna was possessed of a highly-developed sense of self that suffered greatly under his provincial existence in Mantua. For 15 ducats per month, food and lodging for six persons, and the necessary firewood, the brother-in-law of Giovanni Bellini served as court painter to Lodovico Gonzaga (1412–1478). In 1460, after long hesitation, he left Padua, where he had made a name for himself as a painter (his masterwork in the Erimitani Church was largely destroyed in the Second World War), and took up residence in his new refuge, Mantua. The city's reputation as a center of culture had traveled far beyond its borders because no lesser figures than Donatello, Alberti, Laurana, Fancelli, Ariosto, and Torquato Tasso frequented the palace that gradually developed into the greatest in Italy. Mantegna served three generations of the Gonzaga family; and when the Duchess Isabella d'Este (d. 1539), an enthusiastic collector and patron of the arts, opened her salon and engaged in an exchange of letters with the cultural greats of the age, Mantegna was still in Mantua.

Isabella set the social pattern for the ladies of her epoch. Her informal elegance corresponded precisely with the ideas of a writer like Baldassare Castiglione, whose *Il Libro del Cortegiano* (The Book of the Courtier, 1528) described the ideal courtier—the Renaissance man, or *uomo universale*. The book enumerates and details the prevailing forms of appearance of fashion and education that have continued to be held up as criteria for success until this day: education, humor, and a dynamic manner.

In spite of the cultural blossoming of the city, Mantegna believed his genius was constantly undervalued, and conveyed his discontent in many a letter to his patrons. In fact, Lodovico Gonzaga demanded more of his artists than the production of glorious frescoes and panels; he also set them tasks beneath the dignity of the trained artist: "I wish you to draw me two lifelike guinea fowl, a cock and a hen, and send the drawing here to me,

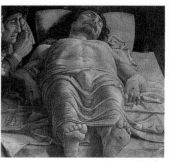

Andrea Mantegna, *Dead Christ*, ca. 1480. Tempera on canvas, 25¾ x 31½ inches (66 x 81 cm). Pinacoteca di Brera, Milan. Mantegna's preference for extreme foreshortening, even in pictures with the holiest of themes, disturbed many of his contemporaries. The monumentalization and revolutionary reduction to the central motif becomes even more striking in comparison with the young Carpaccio's treatment of the same theme.

Vittore Carpaccio, *Preparation of Christ for the Grave*, ca. 1505. Oil on canvas, 56½ x 72 inches (145 x 185 cm). Gemäldegalerie, Berlin.

because I want my carpet-makers to weave it for me. You can see the guinea fowl in the garden at Mantua," wrote Lodovico to the master in 1469. At times such demands proved more than Mantegna was willing to bear, as in 1480 when the Duke of Milan sent some drawings to Federico Gonzaga with the request that Mantegna render them as miniatures. Mantegna was visibly insulted, and Gonzaga himself had to greet Sforza with empty hands; he could only reply by forwarding his artist's strident objection that the duke's request was "rather a task for a mere book illustrator than for him, because he is not accustomed to painting small figures."

Andrea Mantegna, *Camera degli Sposi* (ceiling detail), 1465–1474. Fresco, Palazzo Ducale, Mantua. Mantegna was the first to create an illusionistic ceiling fresco with figures who look down vertically upon the observer. This work provided the impulse for the perspectival ceiling painting of the following centuries.

Mantegna's fresco cycle in the small *Camera degli Sposi* of the ducal palace is one of the most successful compositions of the epoch in its treatment of space and perspective. This masterpiece presents a combination of scenes from courtly life, portraits, and important events in the history of the family of Lodovico Gonzaga, all set in an imaginary garden pavillion opening onto a wide landscape. The painting of the arched ceiling is done in *trompe-l'oeil* technique and creates the illusion of an opening through which several ladies are gazing down; on the balustrade is a peacock, and *putti* are hanging playfully onto the railing.

Donatello's sojourn in Padua and Andrea del Catagno's in Venice left unmistakable traces in the work of Mantegna. The statue-like plasticity, the pronounced corporality, and the monumental presence of his figures are much closer to the ideals of the Florentine school than to those of the Venetian. Mantegna cultivated, furthermore, a deep love for antiquity and its arts. He devoted far more attention to the treasures of the ancient Roman Empire than to the richness of nature, which was, of course, esteemed by many other Renaissance artists as the highest teacher of the arts.

With this predilection for the antique, Mantegna also set his *St. Sebastian* in the midst of ancient ruins, studded with fragments of sculpture. The artist's signature appears in Greek characters behind the broken column to the left. Sebastian here seems to be presented neither as the patron of archers, nor as the patron saint of Rome, but possibly as a protector from the plague (as a successor to Apollo) that repeatedly afflicted the cities of Italy.

According to Vasari, there was one further and very particular effect evoked by the liveliness of the beautiful and naked young man: If the portrait were hung in a church, then the monks surely noticed that "women were aroused to sinful thoughts at the sight of the attractive and sensual representation of life."

Andrea Mantegna, *St. Sebastian*, ca. 1460. Tempera on wood, 26½ x 11¾ inches (68 x 30 cm). Kunsthistorisches Museum, Vienna.

The court and art of the Ferrara family

Even more strongly than their Gonzaga relations in Mantua, the Estes had close ties to the most influential families of their time. The three brothers Leonello, Borso, and Ercole I succeeded each other in Ferrara— and even their names reflect the extravagent taste of their father. The "Little Lion" was followed by Borso, a namesake of one of the knights of King Arthur's Round Table, and finally by "Hercules." Their sisters, graced with similarly fanciful names, married into the Sforza, Malatesta, Gonzaga, Pico della Mirandola, and Montefeltro clans; half of of the ruling houses of Italy were members of the Este family.

Like the Gonzaga family, the Estes also involved themselves with the arts. If his cousins in Urbino offered a home for masters not only from all of Italy, but also from the Netherlands and Spain, Leonello d'Este commissioned works by Rogier van der Weyden, including the *Deposition from the Cross* (see p. 58). Leonello also engaged the services of Pisanello, Jacopo Bellini, Alberti, and Piero della Francesca. The uniqueness in the approach of the Ferrara, however, is rooted far more in the local tradition, which reached its high point with Cosmè Tura (ca. 1430–1495).

Cosmè Tura, *Pietà*, ca. 1470. Oil and tempera on canvas, 18¾ x 12¾ inches (48 x 33 cm). Museo Correr, Venice.

Considering the style of this official court painter, the first question that comes to mind is what on earth the Este family had in mind by having the prospective "marriage" portraits of their nubile daughters done by this particular painter. Tura's hallmark is his knotty expressionism. Every detail is angular, pointed, and harsh. But, in fact, it is exactly this approach that brings out the beauty in his tender and melancholy female figures.

Under Tura's direction—along with advice from the Humanist-astrologist Pellegrino Prisciani (ca. 1435–1516)—one of the most extraordinary of the secular fresco cycles of the *Quattrocento* came into being: the Hall of the Months in the Palazzo Schifanoia ("palace for those disgusted by boredom") was produced by various painters, including Francesco del Cossa (ca. 1436–1478) and Ercole de' Roberti (ca. 1450–1496). Because of the economic orientation of Borso d'Este's appreciation of art—he preferred to pay for paintings by the square foot—the wisest aproach for painters was to cover all four walls with frescoes. But the payment and respect their works earned seemed nonetheless to have been less than satisfactory, for Cossa wrote a letter of complaint to the duke: "I am Francesco del Cossa, who single-handedly painted three surfaces in the antechamber." He continues, he is not just anyone and feels he has been "treated and judged and equipped like the sorriest apprentice in Ferarra."

Ercole de' Roberti, *Pietà*, 1482–1486. Oil on canvas, 29½ x 19 inches (76 x 49 cm). Walker Art Gallery, Liverpool.

The frescoes depict the twelve months. Each is divided into three superimposed fields portraying (from top to bottom) the triumphal procession of a god, the sign of the zodiac with representatives of the three monthly decans (three units of ten days within each month), and finally, scenes from the life of Borso d'Este. In the course of the year, the acts of the duke are revealed: "We are standing here in front of a self-portrait of the state which presents its tasks, its role, its duties, its ideals and its models before the eyes of the public" (Ranieri Varese).

We know of Leonello that he loved to select the color of his clothing according to the constellation of the planets. In 1912, art historian Aby Warburg had used detective work to trace the origin of those rakish, exotic, and elegant personifications of the decans surrounding the signs of the zodiac back to Orient lands.

The month *April* presents the triumph of Venus as the goddess of love, before whom the chained war god Mars is kneeling. In reality, the scene is the ingenious transposition of a courtly topos: The knight is chained by love to a venerable lady, who graciously rewards his admiration. Warburg even traces Mars back to the Nordic legend of Lohengrin, the "Swan Knight" of Arthurian legend, from which the namesake of Borso also derives.

The zodiacal sign of the bull decorates the middle band of the painting, surrounded by three divinities, each responsible for ten days of the month: A young woman with a child, a man with a turban and a key, and a warrior outfitted with with an arrow, accompanied by a dragon, a horse, and a dog.

Francesco del Cossa, *April*, (illustration of month), ca. 1470. Fresco, width 4 feet (124 cm), Sala dei mesi, Palazzo Schifanoia, Ferrara.
The chariot of the goddess is pulled by swans and surrounded by young lovers who are taking their pleasure among the rabbits in a blooming meadow. The Three Graces in the background lend classical legitimation to their activities. With their musical instruments, the elegant company provides the harmony necessary for the young man (right foreground) to slip his hand between the legs of his beloved.

Francesco Francia, *Sacra Conversazione*, ca. 1494. Altar panel, San Giacomo Maggiore, Bologna.

Carlo Crivelli, *Annunciation with St. Ermidius*, 1486. Tempera on wood, transferred to canvas, 80¾ x 57⅛ inches (207 x 147 cm). National Gallery, London.

In the bottom band of the fresco we finally approach earthly realms. The duke, returning home from the hunt, gives his court fool the gift of a coin—an act over which the miserly duke must make a grimace. In the background, in the form of a frieze honoring the patron saint of the city, the Palio di San Giorgio at the Church of San Sebastiano is portrayed along the border.

In the long run, Ferrara was too small for three such extravagant artists as Tura, Cossa, and Roberti; thus, after 1470, we discover Cossa and Roberti as founders of a painting academy in Bologna. They were soon joined by pupils of Tura: Lorenzo Costa (1460–1535), who worked intensively with Francesco Francia (ca. 1450–1517) in Bologna, and after 1506 became the court painter in Mantua—Mantegna's successor, so to speak. Like Mantegna, Costa remained faithful to the Gonzaga family until the end of his life.

The northern Italian cities of Bologna, Ferrara, and Mantua found themselves caught in the culturally rich but geographically tense field between Florence and Venice. The Bolognese Francesco Raibolini, known as Francia, devoted himself totally to secular art and was an exemplary link between the style of Venice (Vivarini, Bellini), which was oriented on coloration, and the painting of Tuscany, whose strength was based on drawing and plasticity (Signorelli, Perugino). Naturally, the Florentines, who saw themselves as the inventors of

With their metallic character, Crivelli's richly decorated works derive life from a mixture of sweet naivety and sharply-lined drawing, in which they clearly reveal the influence of Tura. The abundant decorative details and rich festoons relegate the sacred subject matter to the background.

the Renaissance, looked down upon everyone else. One of Vasari's telling anecdotes reports that the highly respected Florentine master Francia suffered a stroke while he was unpacking a painting by Raphael that had been sent to him from Rome for safekeeping, and died shortly thereafter. The famed Florentine sense of self-worth could hardly be expressed more graphically than by this anecdote.

Giovanni Santi's hymn of praise to artists

1494 marks the death of Giovanni Santi, who earned a place in art history for two services: He fathered Raphael, and composed a poem in which he named the painters he thought were the most important of his age. Such a window into the past is always interesting, and Santi's names yield insight into the evaluation of the time period which, amazingly, still (or again) corresponds largely with our current evaluation.

Because Santi lived in Urbino, his list is not determined by local metropolitan patriotisms. Only his particular admiration for contemporary Melozzo da Forli (1438–1494) probably arises from Santi's own stylistic roots, which he saw as perfected in Melozzo. Santi reveals himself through his knowledge of the Netherlanders, whose art he encountered in Urbino, but also through his knowledge of the qualities of Venetian painting. His openness to the work of his own and the succeeding generation

Melozzo da Forli, *Angels Playing Music* (detail), 1464. Fresco, Pinacoteca, Vatican, Rome.

is clear in his inclusion of younger colleagues such as Ghirlandaio, Perugino, Leonardo, Signorelli, Lippi, and Botticelli. His poem begins with Mantegna, and ends:
"In this art, at once gleaming and noble, there have been so many illuminated figures in our century, that all other periods seem contemptible./ In Bruges the most valued was / the great van Eyck and his pupil Rogier / under many others, gifted with perfection / in this art, and the highest mastery / of coloration were so complete / that they surpassed reality on many occasions. / However, also there in present-day Italy / there are the worthy Gentile da Fabriano, / Fra Giovanni Angelico of Fiesole, glowing for goodness. / And in minting coins and in painting, there is Pisanello, /Fra Lippo Lippi, and Fransesco Pesellino, / Domenico, known as the Venetian, / Masaccio, Andrea del Castagno, Paolo Uccello, / Antonio and Piero Pollaiulol, who are great draftsmen. / Piero della Francesca, who is older than these others, and / two youths, both in talent and in years: / Leonardo da Vinci and Piero Perugino / from Pieve—what a divine painter! / Ghirlandaio and the young Filippino Lippi, / Sandro Botticelli; from Cortona / Luca Signorelli, a talented soul with a unique spirit. / Then, on the other side of that beautiful land of Etruria / Antonello da Messina, a gleaming man, / Giovanni Bellini, whose fame is widely spread, / Gentile his brother, Cosmè Tura, and as his counterpart / Ercole de' Roberti, and many more that I do not mention. / But I will not omit Melozzo da Forli, who is dear to me / and who has accomplished so much with perspective."

German masters

As Italy readied itself to step into the High Renaissance, and all the technical and artistic achievements of the 15th century stood available to artists like a bank account to be drawn from for the journey, the scene north of the Alps seemed more static. If there was less movement, however, the landscape continued to glitter with the creation of Late Gothic jewels. Under the particular influences of the age, outstanding artists were producing works of extraordinary power.

Nineteenth-century Renaissance historians concerned themselves primarily with Italian artists. In 1900, for example, James Weale, the biographer of the painter Gerard David (ca. 1463–1523), could only lament in frustration that knowledge of the various northern schools was still very incomplete. A few artists, however, stood out from the general darkness.

A good deal was known about David's teacher, for example, the Flemish artist Hans Memling (ca. 1440–1494). His name first appears in 1465 in the city registry of Bruges as Jan van Mimnelinghe from Seligenstadt, a small city on the Main River known for its venerable Benedictine abbey. He carried his German identity with him through his life, appearing in annals variously as "Meester Hans" or even as "the German Hans." As for Arnolfini and Portinari (see p. 56 and 59), it was wealthy families of Italian origin, now living for commercial reasons in northern Europe, who tended to commission portraits and altars. Memling, too, created his most significant work for Angelo Tani, an Italian representative of the Medici family who lived in Bruges.

see p. 56 and 59

1435
First copper engravings supercede the woodcut
1450
Gutenberg sets up his printing press in Mainz
1455
Beginning of the struggle between the Houses of York and Lancaster for the English throne (War of the Roses)

Dieric Bouts, *Last Judgment, Fall into Hell* (detail), 1468–1470. Oil on wood, 44 x 26½ inches (113 x 68 cm). Musée des Beaux-Arts, Lille. Louvain's official painter cultivated a subtle application of color and a filigree-like wealth of detail. Only the side panels of his altar (*Fall into Hell* and *Procession of the Saints*) have survived.

Memling's *Last Judgment* was the outgrowth of a competition with the painter Dieric Bouts (ca. 1420–1475). The Netherlander had in 1468 also begun a painting with the same theme. Upon completion, Memling's work was intended to be shipped, probably under Burgundian flag, to Italy, but instead fell into the hands of a pirate licensed by the city of Danzig, who carried it back to his native city. The *Danzig Chronicle* from 1473 remarks: "Item. Last Tuesday after Easter Paul Benke captured a galleon with a great hook"; a later entry adds: "On this galleon was a panel which has been set on St. George's Junker altar, a beautiful, noble, and artful painting, recently finished."

ca. 1465–1536
Erasmus of Rotterdam, Humanist
1466
Casimir IV of Poland defeats Teutonic Knights
1469
Hanseatic League wages sea war against England
1470
Rudolf Agricola's treatise *De formando studio* spurs the study of Humanism in Germany
1477
Maximilian I marries Maria of Burgundy, gaining the Netherlands for the Hapsburg crown
1481
Inquisition begins in Spain
1483
Charles VIII ascends the French throne
1487
The Hammer of Witchcraft by the papal inquisitors launches witch-hunting trials
1492
Alexander VI becomes pope
1493
Maximilian I elected German Emperor; first peasant uprisings in Alsace
1494
Ship of Fools, rhymed writings against human weaknesses, by Brant
1498
Louis XII becomes king of France

Hans Memling, *Last Judgment* (center panel, triptych), 1466–1473. Oil on wood, 86 x 62½ inches (221 x 160 cm). Nationalmuseum, Danzig.

The central picture of Memling's painting portrays the traditional image of Christ as Judge of the World, and also St. Michael, who is weighing a good soul against a bad. While this conception of judgment must certainly be understood symbolically, the figures seem at first glance to be portrayed with such a radical naturalism that symbolic interpretation becomes difficult. For how can justice rule when there is no generally valid measure, and one soul can be arbitrarily weighed against another? Furthermore, the judgments pronounced by Christ can hardly be binding, when the angels and the devil are still fighting for the soul between them, irrespective of Christ's decision. Such an arbitrary interpretation of the process of the Last Judgment conveyed by medieval illustrations must have seemed not only threatening to the Renaissance, but also irritating in its lack of logic. Italy, therefore, soon developed a convincing solution to the problems of the content of such paintings (see p. 120).

In Memling's painting, the scene expands in all directions: Upward to the rows of saints surrounding Christ, downward to the endless depths of Hell, and horizontally into a soft rolling landscape where a few latecomers are still arising from their graves. The male figures are at least provided with various heads—old, young, bearded, tonsured. But the absolute similarity of their young, slim bodies comes as a surprise, as if the artist relied on the same model throughout. The same holds true for the females, all of whom sport oval, well-proportioned features and long red hair. This schematization is symptomatic of the lack of innovation in Netherlandish art in the final third of the 15th century.

Germany, the land through which everyone had to travel on their way from the Netherlands to Italy, or from Prague to Burgundy or Paris, was not

Martin Schongauer, *Incense Vessel.* Undated, copper engraving. Staatliche Kunsthalle, Karlsruhe.

left untouched by the
innovative tendencies,
though the develop-
ments made there
were more moderate
than in Italy. German
art consciously
attempted to fuse the
Gothic inheritance
with the new style
from the south. Far
more than in Italy,
where a continuity
with medieval art was
undesired, Germany
consciously preserved
certain traditions,
especially in the area
of religious art.

Michel Pacher, *Saints Augustine and Gregory*, Altar of the Church Fathers Neustift (center panel), ca. 1483. Oil on wood. 80½ x 76½ inches (206 x 196 cm). Alte Pinakothek, Munich.

Michael Pacher (ca. 1435–1498), who was probably familiar with the work of the Italians, and especially those of Mantegna, succeeded in devoting a (Renaissance) painting, replete with perspective and the naturalistic arrangement of figures, to the spirit of the Late Gothic.

Next to Pacher, the most striking exemplar of the combination is Martin Schongauer (ca. 1450–1491), born the son of an Augsburg goldsmith in Colmar. Through his selection of prototypes, he oriented himself more toward the north, especially to the Netherlandish circle around Rogier van de Weyden. Although his was the most important painting workshop in upper Germany, only one painting can be ascribed to him with certainty—*Madonna in the Rose Arbor* (Martin's Church, Colmar). His copper engravings, however, were brought into many workshops, which valued his designs as patterns, models, and inspirations. He is rather the outstanding conclusion to a south-German Gothic tradition—master E.S., master of house books—that is, a revolutionary within his field.

Tilman Riemenschneider, *Altar of the Twelve Messengers* (detail), before 1509. Lindenholz, Kurpfälzisches Museum, Heidelberg. A meditative peace and finely detailed organization characterize the introverted *ouevre* of Riemenschneider. Although produced at the moment of transition from the Early to the High Renaissance, his work cultivates its Gothic roots with great sensibility.

Tilman Riemenschneider (ca. 1460–1531) and Veit Stoss (ca. 1447–1533)

The sculptor Tilman Riemenschneier shared the fate of many of his northern European colleagues: He was forgotten immediately after his death. Not until 1822, when street-repair work near the Cathedral of Würzburg uncovered the gravestone erected by his son, did he emerge into the light of history. Riemenschneider had in fact spent almost his entire life in Würzburg, having entered the Lucas Guild (sculptors) in 1483. Two years later, he married the widow of a goldsmith, a union that brought him many advantages, for only a married man could take on apprentices to train in his workshop. Furthermore, as the husband of the widow of a master, he himself ascended immediately to the rank of master—and only as master did a man acquire the full rights of citizenship. Riemenschneider was not alone in pursuing such a path to prosperity: Reuland Frueauf the Younger (d. 1497) established himself as a painter in Passau in the same way.

Riemenschneider eventually established himself at the head of a large household. He married three more times after the death of his first wife, and achieved renown as a craftsman and social respect as councilman in and mayor of Würzburg. Personal conflicts with the clergy, however, as well as his marked sense of justice, led him in 1525 to support the rebels who set themselves against the privileges of the nobility and clergy in the Peasants' War. The urban citizenry also used the struggle of the peasants to claim rights for themselves. After the revolt was suppressed, its supporters were banned from the city council, and part of their property was confiscated. Some of the supporters were executed; others, including Riemenschneider, were imprisoned and tortured.

Although he survived his punishment, the defeat of the revolt was a personal humiliation from which Riemenschneider never recovered. His sculpture in any case stands rather as the apotheosis of the strain of the medieval-melancholic in German art than as a vital start in a new direction, and his work was increasingly alien to the new age. The Reformation largely eliminated contracts for altars; this, combined with his economic decline, led Riemenschneider to withdraw into silence well before the end of his life.

The sculptor Veit Stoss, who lived and worked chiefly in Nuremberg, dared a similar stylistic balancing act between the Gothic and Renaissance. His abandonment of Nuremberg for service in the court of King Kasimir in Cracow may have aroused jealousy among his compatriots; in any case, he was forced to pay a high price upon his return. For an infringement against the money conversion ordinances and a disagreement with the city council, he was sentenced to have his cheeks bored through by a hot poker.

Like his contemporary Riemenschneider, after suffering torture and humiliation, Stoss emerged a broken man. He fled to Männerstadt, but even the support and political rehabilitation provided by Emperor Maximilian I was unable to dilute his bitterness.

Veit Stoss, *Christ as a Man of Sorrows*, 1499–1505. Wood, St. Sebald, Nuremberg. The characteristic faces and figures of Stoss's striking sculptures are draped in living, sweeping garments. The bodies beneath seem to be fluidly formed without, however, disguising the Gothic tradition of German art.

Rise of the Lagoon Republic

The former Byzantine province of Venice had achieved political independence at an early date. In 1204 the venerable old Doge Enrico Dandolo had provided impressive proof of the city's self-sufficiency. After a series of adroit diplomatic moves, Venice exploited the opportunity of a crusade to quickly reconquer the renegade city of Zara on the way to the Holy Land and subsequently to destroy Constantinople. The double victory also won Venice the necessary respect from the West that allowed the city to pursue its own course.

Culturally, however, Venice long remained under Eastern influence. Even the names of its churches reflect the customs of Byzantine culture: Contrary to Western tradition, the names derive from holy figures of the Old Testament, such as San Giobbe (Job), San Moise, or San Zaccaria. In architecture, especially dome construction, in icon painting, and in mosaic work (whose extinction was officially ascertained in 1424), the arts of the old Byzantine metropolis continued to live on in Venice. Florentine experts in perspective including Paolo Uccello and Filippo Lippi and sculptors such as Donatello and Verocchio were lured to the city and contributed to the renewal of Venetian art, from which such masters as Carpaccio and Mantegna drew long-term benefit.

The influence of the Vatican was far weaker in Venice than in other Italian cities. San Marco was the city church of Venice, and was built and fitted out by the Serenissima. In contrast, the location of the bishop's church clearly indicated the merely peripheral significance of the papal representative: San Pietro stood behind the armory, far from the economic and political centers of the city, the Rialto and the Piazza of San Marco.

Not only did numerous Venetian churches maintain their own rich traditions quite independent of the influence of the Vatican, even the Renaissance movement itself inspired few real innovations in sacred architecture during the course of the *quattrocento*. One

The Cornerstone of Venice's Fame

of the first truly Renaissance-inspired buildings erected in Venice is the cemetery church of Marco Codussi (ca. 1440–1505). Constructed entirely of white Istrian stone, the facade is distinguished by a geometry based on the circle and the square, and thus brings a new rational clarity to the architecture of the city. The antique-style masonry extending from the pilasters is a novelty that for many years remained the sole example of such stonework in Venice.

Mauro Codussi, Facade of San Michele, started 1468. Venice.

Codussi was the great competitor of the Lombardi, a family of architects and sculptors who operated an influential workshop in the city. The rivalry for important contracts was not always conducted by fair means. Thus in 1491 a commission suddenly ended Lombardi participation on an important project that was headed by the artists Codussi and Antonio Rizzo. Subsequently, the Lombardos received fewer commissions. In 1498, however, Pietro Lombardo succeeded Rizzo as the foreman of the work on the doge's palace after Rizzo was forced to flee Venice, presumably as the result of one of the innumerable Venetian internecine intrigues.

Pietro at this point handed over the family workshop to his son Tullio in order to devote himself to his new responsibilities at the palace and, after the death of Codussi, the Lombardo family workshop attained a position of uncontested leadership—an achievement that in turn immediately called down upon their heads sanctions of the jealous sculptors' guild. Finally, however, the withdrawal of Tullio's brother from the workshop led to its decline after 1506: It proved impossible for Tullio to run the family business successfully by himself.

Vittore Carpaccio, *St. George Presenting the Dragon*, 1502–1507. Oil on canvas, 55 x 140 inches (141 x 360 cm). Scuola di San Giorgio, Venice.

Vittore Carpaccio (ca. 1460/65–1523/26)

When Italian artists lashed out against the abundance of detail in northern art (see p. 67), one can only wonder what they had to say about the works of Vittore Carpaccio, who seemingly wasted his rich talents on paintings of drying laundry, exotic birds, bizarre headwear, and decaying corpses. His paintings were never intended, however, to overwhelm with a first, overpowering impression, but to press the observer to make a stroll of discovery through gardens, courtyards, bays, and buildings.

Carpaccio, a native Venetian, was considerably younger than his famous colleagues (and teachers) Gentile and Giovanni Bellini. His fine linear design and strong formal order were true to the ideals of the early Renaissance. He fitted out three *scuole*, or lay fraternities, in Venice (Scuola di Sant'Orsola, di San Giorgio, and degli Albanesi). His fascination with theatrical, oriental costuming is clearly evident in his illustrations for the Legend of Saint George, leading scholars to conclude that Carpaccio must have traveled at least as far as Dalmatia to have met this exuberant variety of exotic forms. In 1500 Venice was still a leading mercantile power, engaged in lively trade with the East. Carpaccio's aged teacher Gentile Bellini had even been sent by the doge to Constantinople to do a portrait of Sultan Muhammed II. The economically and culturally profitable contact with the "heathens" had always come easier to the Venice than to the other Italian city-states, who felt, for a variety of motives, bound to the pope.

Alvise Vivarini (ca. 1445–1503/05)

The largest state commissions of the late 15th and early 16th centuries undoubtedly were garnered by the Bellini family. But, in addition to the Bellini, there were a number of painters, quite highly admired by their contemporaries, whose work also earns respect today: Alvise Vivarini, Marco Basaiti (active 1496–1530), Giovanni Cima da Conegliano (1459/60–ca, 1517/18).

Vivarini was born in Venice as the son of a painter. Although his painting at times is rather wooden, and only his late works are warmed by the Bellinis' power of illumination, Vivarini's workshop nonetheless produced a series of pieces that reveal him as a vital representative of the Venetian art of his age.

Only at the end of the 15th century, when all the technical developments in the area of the arts—whose invention the Venetians had left to others—had drawn to its close, was Venice able to find its own creative identity, and in a few decades developed into a leading and innovative art metropolis. The Venetian atmosphere, the shimmering of light above the lagoon, was the "nature" whose imitation artists like the Bellinis, masters of the possibilities offered by oil painting, strove for, and at the beginning of the 16th century accomplished: "In the moment that one learns to paint air and water, the first painterly forces that strike a tone of their own begin to move in the city of the Lagoon" (Harald Keller). In contrast to Florence, where *disegno*, drawing, was seen as the fundamental principle behind all the graphic arts, Venetian painting thrived from its own unique feel for color, an understanding that apparently was passed on in the workshops and survived through the centuries, from Bellini, through Veronese, to Tiepolo.

Alvise Vivarini and Marco Basaiti, *Panel of St. Ambrosius*, ca. 1495–1503. Wood, Santa Maria Gloriosa dei Frari, Venice.

The attribution of the *Saint Ambrosius* panel to Carpaccio (by Vasari) and Guarino (by Sansovino, who perhaps simply misread the name "Vivarine" in the inscription) shows how difficult it was, even in the 16th century, to classify a painting stylistically. Apparently Marco Basaiti completed the painting, but what proportion of the work belongs to him is still debated among art historians.

Giovanni Bellini, *Sacra conversazione*, 1505. Oil on wood, transferred to canvas, 195 x 91½ inches (500 x 235 cm). San Zaccaria, Venice. The painting is a pure example of the genre of *sacra conversazione*, meditatively harmonious down to its last detail: The view into the landscape is reduced to two narrow strips, while the floral element is picked up by the artificial movement in the mosaic pattern in the apse, and thus, in turn, enters into a dialogue with the restrained austerity of the tiled floor.

In Venice far more than in Florence, the medieval structure of the workshops remained intact. Thus, painters like Vivarini, Bellini, Tintoretto, Veronese, and Bassano worked in family-operated businesses, as did the Buon and the Lombardi brothers in the fields of sculpture and architecture.

Giovanni Bellini (1427/30–1516)

In contrast to the hard contours and antique style of his brother-in-law Andrea Mantegna, or the precise and abundant details of a Carpaccio, Giovanni Bellini developed a characteristic style of soft and earnest figures whose life arises simply from the intensity of his use of color and from the inner peace of his composition—without urgent reminders of antiquity or exaggerated foreshortening. As the pupil of his father, Jacopo, and brother to Gentile, Giovanni's approach comes as no surprise. He perfected a harmonic balance, employing the soft, warm effects possible with oils in a masterly hand. Giovanni was thus the only painter to make the leap from the Early Renaissance to the High Renaissance within his own work. The Humanist Pietro Bembo characterized him as an artist pleased that "his style stood beyond the set limits, and who is used to pursuing his own ways in painting."

In the course of his long life, Bellini circled around the same concrete subjects, such as the Pietà, redefining the precision of his figures. His panel for San Zaccaria carries the genre of the *sacra conversazione* to its apotheosis: The pictorial space corresponds perfectly with the architecture of the church itself. The figures have stepped back from the foreground ramp, thus conferring a sense of space and air on the painted chapel. The four saints are completely isolated in their tranquil, symmetrical postures; no eye contact disturbs their contemplation. Only the angel at the foot of the very human Madonna peers out of the picture, establishing a connection with the observer.

Giovanni Bellini, *Pietà*, ca. 1467. Tempera on wood, 33½ x 41¾ inches (86 x 107 cm), Pinacoteca di Brera, Milan.

The Tuscan artists are not the only ones whose works created riddles for art historians—and doubtless for their contemporaries as well—the Venetians have also posed intriguing questions. Three works, by Bellini, Giorgione, and Titian, exemplify the puzzling blurring of boundaries between sacred and profane art, or between allegory, genre painting, and mythology.

Bellini's *Holy Allegory* (at times variously ascribed to Giorgione and to Marco Basaiti) depicts individual figures on and around a plastered terrace before a lake and a rocky landscape. The persons obviously include a throned Mary and various saints who have found their way into an unconventional *sacra conversatione*. Whether the work refers to the poem of Guillaume de Deguileville, *Le Pèlerinage de l'âme*, or whether the innocent children are really meant to be souls from Purgatory who have now arrived in Paradise, remains unknown. Whatever might be the motive forces that have brought this group of figures to this remarkable place are not subject to final explanation.

Giovanni Bellini, *Holy Allegory*, ca. 1490–1500. Tempera on wood, 28½ x 46½ inches (73 x 119 cm). Galleria degli Uffizi, Florence. The multilayered coding of theological and humanistic messages—and how little we understand of their meanings today—becomes all too clear as soon as a painting deviates from the customary iconographic figures.

left:
Giovanni Bellini,
Madonna with Child,
1480–1490. Oil on
wood, 35½ x 25⅗ inches
(91 x 65 cm). National
Gallery, London.

right:
Giovanni Cima da
Conegliano, *Madonna
with Child*, undated. Oil
on wood, 26¼ x 20¼
inches (68 x 52 cm).
Städelsches Kunstinsti-
tut, Frankfurt am Main.

Giorgione (1477/78–1510)

A veil of incomprehensibility shrouds both the person
and the works of Bellini's pupil Giorgione. Like his
master, Giorgione steps across the threshold from the
Early Renaissance into the High Renaissance. His
Thunderstorm is probably the single most mysterious
smaller work of Venetian painting. Despite the fact that
no other painter of his time awarded the landscape
such a preeminent position in his work as did
Giorgione himself, in terms of art history, it is very
difficult to imagine a painting without a recognizable
subject—but even the oldest surviving description of
the painting was unable to suggest anything more
complex than a soldier and a gypsy during a thunderstorm (Michiel, 1530). As a result, art historians have
come up with a multitude of proposals (as with Piero
della Francesca's *Scourging*), that were compiled and
expanded by Salvatore Settis in 1978: The figures may
represent Giorgione's family (Burckhardt), the Holy
Family resting on the flight into Egypt (Stange), the
birth of Bacchus (Klauner), the discovery of Moses
(Calvesi), the legend of St. Theodore (De Grummond),
or Adam and Eve (Settis)—to list only a few options.

A second work of Giorgione's that was probably
completed by Titian portrays a *Rural Concert*. Two
young men, one elegantly dressed, the other simply,
sit in the midst of a rolling Arcadian landscape. They

lean slightly toward each other as the elegant young man plays the lute, seemingly unaware of the two naked women, one holding a flute, the other apparently pouring water into a fountain. Are the women courtesans, nymphs, or allegories of the elements—the splashing of the water, the piping of the wind? When Vasari viewed Giorgione's frescoes in Venice at an early date, he observed that the painter had been permitted to compose "wholly at his own whim," in other words, without a specifically assigned theme. The results, according to the early biographer-critic, were merely figures of fantasy: "one finds neither a logical order of images, nor individual incidents drawn from the life of famous persons of antiquity, nor from modern times; for my part, I have never been able to understand the meaning of the whole, and have found no one able to understand it so as to explain it to me." Vasari thus emerges as the grandfather of the desire for a satisfactory explanation for every picture in the history of art.

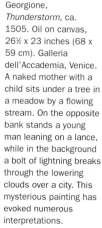

Georgione, *Thunderstorm*, ca. 1505. Oil on canvas, 26½ x 23 inches (68 x 59 cm). Galleria dell'Accademia, Venice. A naked mother with a child sits under a tree in a meadow by a flowing stream. On the opposite bank stands a young man leaning on a lance, while in the background a bolt of lightning breaks through the lowering clouds over a city. This mysterious painting has evoked numerous interpretations.

Giorgione and Titian, *Rural Concert*, 1510/11. Oil on canvas, 41 x 53½ inches (105 x 137 cm). Musée du Louvre, Paris.

Benedetto da Maiano, Palazzo Strozzi, begun in 1489. Florence.

The fortress-like facades of many of the early Renaissance palaces, with their multiple rows of arcaded windows, are an emphatic embodiment of the claim to power and high position of the influential families who built them. Furthermore, they testify to the desire of the nobility to barricade themselves against the growing proletariat of the cities.

A prime example of this type of palace is the *Palazzo Strozzi*, designed by Benedetto da Maiano in Florence (1489–1500, original model by Antonio da Sangallo the Elder). The weight of the massive, rustic-style masonry dissipates toward the top of the building, the height of the stories correspondingly decreases, and the windows, which tend to recede into the massive surfaces of the walls, thus become more dominant and relax the severity of the facade as it rises. The building is crowned by a broad cornice. The palace offers an outstanding example of the house style favored at the time by wealthy and noble families throughout Tuscany.

Within the architectural genre of the fortified house, the most imposing example was naturally the Palazzo Medici-Riccardi. Above the enormous socle of the ground floor with its rusticated stone and windows framed in massive portal arches rise two further stories with twin windows set under round arches. The stone relief becomes less pronounced with each succeeding story, corresponding to the decreasing height of the stories.

The Palazzo Rucellai, designed by Leon Battista Alberti and begun under the direction of Bernardo

Michelozzo di Bartolomeo, Palazzo Medici-Riccardi, 1444–1450. Florence.

Leon Battista Alberti, Palazzo Rucellai, 1446 or later. Florence.

from the Colosseum: Doric, Ionic, and Corinthian.

In Rome, the Casa di Raffaello by Bramante in contrast reduces the three-floored palace design to two strongly contrasting stories. The ground floor even incorporates small shops into the building, as was usual with ancient townhouses. The massively formed rusticated arches of the ground floor support an elegant colonnade of paired columns on the second floor, between which are set narrow balustraded porticos.

No Italian city, however, contained more palaces than Venice. The long economic success of the thousand-year-old republic had resulted in a prosperity that expressed itself in architecture. In particular, the shore of the Grand Canal developed into a unique kind of open-air architectural museum over the course of the centuries.

During the Renaissance, the typically Gothic asymmetrical facade

Rossellino in 1446, must be understood as a conscious counterstroke to the prevailing norms. Rejecting any obvious display of grandeur for its own sake in favor of the antique, Alberti sought his principles in design. The facade is based on a linear grid derived from the classical organizaion of columns familiar

Donato Bramante, Facade of the Casa di Raffaello, ca. 1510. Copperplate engraving by Antonio Lafréry, 1549. British Museum, London.

Pietro Lombardo, Palazzo Dario, begun in 1487. Venice.
Colored incrustations were a hallmark of the Lombardo workshop and corresponded perfectly to the ideas of early Renaissance architects, who oriented themselves on ancient—or seemingly ancient—sheathing.

fell increasingly out of favor. The Palazzo Dario is a prime example of the playfully ornamental surface and finely detailed organization of Venetian architecture. The house belonged to Giovanni Dario, one of the few nonaristocrats permitted to erect a palace on the Grand Canal. As Secretary of the Republic, he had performed a great diplomatic service in arranging peace between Venice and the Turks under Mohammed II. To construct his palace, he probably commissioned Pietro Lombardo as architect. At the head of a large workshop, Lombardo had become the doyen of Venetian architecture.

Lombardo's colleague Mauro Codussi designed the Palazzo Vendramin-Calergi, whose balanced, strongly modeled front was a statement uttered wholly in the classical vocabulary of the Renaissance and brought to full effect by the light of the lagoon. The subtly colored marble facade gently calls attention to the classical rhythmic scheme of alternating closed and opened surfaces typical of Venetian palaces. The double window arches compare with those of the Palazzo Strozzi in Florence—a motif that became the determining factor in the architectural design of the Venetian palace.

The writer Baldassare Castiglione expressed his enthusiastic admiration for a palace that he claimed many found the most beautiful in all of Italy: The Palazzo Ducale in Urbino. Duke Federico da Montefeltro employed two architects for the project. In addition to Francesco

Luciano Laurana, Palazzo Ducale, begun ca. 1454, entire building (below), and inner court (right). Urbino.

Mauro Codussi, Palazzo Vendramin-Calergi, 1481–1509. Venice.

di Giorgio Martini, the duke also appointed the teacher of Bramante, the Dalmatian Luciano Laurana (1420/25–1479). The Palazzo Ducale is the first palace of the Renaissance to entirely exclude all elements reminiscent of medieval fortifications, emphasized by the clear and open organization of its facades and its graceful interior court.

High Renaissance in Italy
Leonardo da Vinci

1494
Charles VIII occupies Italy; start of struggle between France and the Hapsburgs for Italian Peninsula
1503
Julius II becomes pope
1503–1566
Nostradamus, French astrologist
1507
Death of Cesare Borgia
1509
Henry VIII crowned King of England
1513
Leo X, a Medici, becomes pope
1515
Francis I crowned King of France and conquers the Duchy of Milan
1516
Charles I becomes King of Spain, Naples-Sicily, and the Burgundian Netherlands; after 1519 he reigns as German Emperor Charles V
1527
Conquest and plundering of Rome by Imperial mercenaries
1530
Pope Clement VII crowns Charles V Emperor in Bologna
1532
Machiavelli's *The Prince* published

"Not until you are alone are you wholly yourself."
Leonardo da Vinci (1452–1519)

"Leonardo da Vinci—what a profusion of ideas this name awakens in our innermost being! Where is there an art, or where a science, that could not extol him with every right, if not as its creator, then indeed as its most renowned exponent and illustrious discoverer." With these words in 1889, Paul Müller-Walde begins his biography of Leonardo in which the myth of the *uomo universalis*, the genius in all branches of human endeavor, is once more carved in stone. No other artist has had so much written about him as Leonardo da Vinci, and every discovery of a new manuscript—or new attribution, or even supposition—calls forth yet another avalanche of essays.

Leonardo's name was first inscribed in the Lucas Guild (sculptors) in the city of Florence in 1472. A decade later, the master moved to Milan, following the growing trend among Florentine artists to practice their art in other cities. There in the Lombardy region, he received his first important commission from the *Confratelli della Concezione* in 1483 for a monumental altar painting and the gilding of its carved wooden frame. Leonardo's answer was his *Virgin of the Rocks*. In its original opulent frame, the painting's effect was doubtless much deeper, more shadowy and mysterious than it can be today, hanging on the sober wall of a museum.

Leonardo da Vinci, *Virgin of the Rocks*, ca. 1485. Oil on wood, transferred to linen, 78½ x 48 inches (199 x 122 cm). Musée du Louvre, Paris.

It was well-known that Leonardo required a great deal of time to finish a work, and that he researched it like one possessed. In reality, every new contract seemed burdensome to him at the start, because it meant tying himself down to a commitment. It is therefore hardly surprising that Leonardo procrastinated in carrying out his commissions, or did not even take them up in the first place. Thus, his *Mona Lisa* accompanied him from Milan to the court of Francis I in France. According to Vasari, Francesco del Giocondo commissioned Leonardo to paint a portrait of his wife, Mona Lisa. The patron never received the finished product, however, and after Leonardo's death, the painting became the property of the king of France.

Leonardo da Vinci, *Mona Lisa*, ca. 1500/2. Oil on wood, 30¼ x 21 inches (77 x 53 cm). Musée du Louvre, Paris.

Again and again questions have been raised about whether the *Mona Lisa* was really commissioned by Giocondo—and the myths surrounding the painting became correspondingly more imaginative. The lady with her famous smile is sitting in front of a balustrade on which two columns were probably originally visible to the right and left (the bases are just barely recognizable). Behind her opens a landscape executed in *sfumato*, an atmospheric technique at which Leonardo was an unrivaled master, creating a sense of great depth using a wide spectrum of colors. The same soft corporeality and the inner glow of tender skin may also be found in his portrait of *Ginevra da'Benci*, a famed beauty of the day, whose portrait was painted by several artists. The likeness produced by Leonardo conveys an almost photographic naturalism, which indicates that the artist had already devoted a good deal of study to physical phenomena and to profound reflection on the ideals of beauty.

In addition to large numbers of drafts for war machines, fortifications, flying contraptions, self-propelled vehicles, and clocks to which Leonardo increasingly devoted himself, the artist's posthumous papers contain many nature studies, the most striking of which are his investigations of human anatomy. They are reflected in his creative works in the anatomical construction of

Leonardo da Vinci, *Ginevra de' Benci*, ca. 1474. Oil on wood, 15¼ x 14½ inches (39 x 37 cm). National Gallery of Art, Washington.

Leonardo da Vinci, *Anatomical Study of a Skull*, ca. 1489. Quill and ink over charcoal, 7¼ x 5¼ inches (18.7 x 13.5 cm). Royal Library, Windsor Castle.

Lorenzo di Credi, *Annunciation* (detail), ca. 1480. Oil on wood, 34⅓ x 27½ inches (88 x 71 cm). Galleria degli Uffizi, Florence.

Leonardo's figures and the soundness of their movement. His ideal of beauty was one of natural elegance and graceful flexibility—the antithesis of an exaggerated musculature. Thus he warns his fellow artists: "Do not make all the muscles of your figures visible; even when they are positioned correctly, they should not stand out when the limbs to which they belong are not exerting great force. Furthermore, the limbs and parts of the body that are not performing a function should display no muscles—and if you go about it differently, then you end up depicting a sack of nuts rather than a human body." With amusing formulations such as this, Leonardo took to task a number of his colleagues, in particular Michelangelo, who had a weakness for such well-trained "sacks of nuts."

Some artists, whose names in fact turn up repeatedly in the history of art and whose works are represented in many important museums and churches, nonetheless lived out their existence in the shadow of their better-known and more colorful colleagues. This was true of both Giovanni Cima da Conegliano, who belonged to the circle around the Bellinis, and Lorenzo de Credi (1456/57–1537), a workshop comrade of Leonardo da Vinci and the prize pupil of Verrocchio. The clear contours of Credi's figures hint at his original training as a goldsmith; the figures derive their life, however, from their luminous colors. In his *Annunciation*, the coloration of the figures is countered by the ceramic-like engraved Renaissance architecture in the background. The socle of the wall, rendered in gray-on-gray tones, depicts the creation of Eve, the fall from grace, and the banishment of the first parents from the

Garden of Paradise. Then with Mary, the new Eve, the sins of humankind that had begun with Eve are reconciled and forgiven.

Piero di Cosimo (1462–1521) shared a fate similar to that of Lorenzo de Credi. Although it was hardly unusual for a student to take on the name of his master, the practice came harder to Piero as an apprentice to Cosimo Rosselli than to many others. The curse of bearing the name of a mediocre artist weighed heavily on Piero, just as his openness toward his colleagues' works gave him a reputation as an imitator and even a plagiarist.

In the Florence of Lorenzo de' Medici, Piero came into contact with the writings of Ficino and Poliziano, read Boccaccio, and developed into a specialist in mythological pictures. In many respects he resembled Leonardo: "He was a friend of loneliness and knew no greater pleasure than to lose himself in his own thoughts, and build castles in the air" (Vasari). But, unlike his famed colleague, Piero did not concern himself enough with his career, for only those who made a name for themselves during their lifetimes had the chance to be honored by the world later, or to be rediscovered: "If Piero had been less withdrawn, and if he had looked after himself more in the course of his life than he in fact did, then the greatness of his spirit would have become obvious, and people would have worshipped him; but now he is accounted a fool because of his bestial life, although in the end he harmed no one but himself."

Piero di Cosimo, *Venus, Mars and Amor*, ca. 1505. Oil on wood, 28 x 71 inches (72 x 182 cm). Gemäldegalerie, Berlin.
While the war god Mars has fallen asleep, various *amoretti* are playing with pieces of his armor. The two doves are billing because Venus, the goddess of love, has just awakened. Amor, who is calling Venus's attention to her sleeping lover, seems to want to use the peaceful hours to his advantage.

Laocoön Group, 1st century B.C.? Marble, Museo Pio-Clementino, Vatican, Rome. "To the Humanists, history did not appear as a single continuous process, but rather provided a disconnected mass of material from which one could pick out relatively isolated events and periods for study, and skip over everything that seemed uninteresting or irrelevant." Felix Gilbert, *Das Geschichtsinteresse der Renaissance* (Historical Interests in the Renaissance).

The acceptance of ancient artistic norms reached its apotheosis under the colorful Pope Julius II who, through the aegis of his architect Donato Bramante, established a statuary courtyard in the Vatican itself, the geographical heart of Christianity. The collection displayed to the public the most imposing works of antique classical sculpture. The core of the collection was the group sculpture of Laocoön and his sons, which had been rediscovered in 1506. The physical presence of this "heathen" sculpture had an impact on contemporary artists and on Christian art that cannot be overestimated.

But did the ancient classic influence really effect a substitution of profane for religious content in Renaissance art, or is it rather our own understanding of Christianity that is unable to integrate the worldly and the rational with religiosity?

In Renaissance architecture, the clarity of numbers and the geometrical proportions of the human body had already been accepted as reflections of divinity. By the same reasoning, the worldly variety of images offered by painting and sculpture could be seen as an expression of the existence of God. Thus, to the understanding of many Renaissance thinkers and artists, if God is present in all created things, then the inherent beauty of ancient works of art in no way contradicts the worship of the Christian God. Just as ancient philosophy had already been reconciled with Christian faith, the terms "ancient" and "modern" were by no means incompatible.

Leading examples of this new understanding are the artists Pier Jacopo Alari-Bonacolsi (ca. 1460–1528), who adopted the pseudonym *Antico* in his role as artist, and Galeazzo Mondella (1467–1528), who similarly dubbed himself *Moderno*. Both distinguished themselves through their relentless cultivation of the ancient in their works and through the polished surfaces of their productions, which were sometimes gilded.

Pier Jacopo Alari-Bonacolsi, known as Antico, *Meleager*, late 15th century. Bronze, height 12 inches (30.7 cm). Victoria and Albert Museum, London.

Whereas Antico's *Meleager* clearly presents us with a hero of old, Moderno's *The Scourging of Christ* harks back to ancient Christian iconography. Christ stands against the whipping post in a Laocoön-like posture. Against a background of antique ruins, Roman soldiers contend in an ancient battle scene. The tormenter on the right, who is in the act of striking Christ, stems directly from the group of tyrannocides, the oldest political monument in Greek history. These classical Greek references are not restricted to the merely formal. As priest of Apollo, the soothsayer Laocoön died, together with his sons, for prophesying the truth. In the Renaissance, he personified both suffering and the beginning of a new era in which

Aeneas would leave the destruction of Troy in order to found Rome. The parallels to Christ were clear and, for those knowledgable in art, perfectly logical. The antique world was clearly relevant to the present day—so much so that it almost seemed as if the terms "ancient" and "modern" had become synonymous, or at least sufficiently interwoven to make disentanglement impossible. The antique style lent a greater authenticity to the theme: Christ was, after all, also an ancient figure.

Finally, the Counter-Reformation attempted a line of demarcation between past and present in order to eliminate the "heathen" elements and references from Christianity, and to give primacy to the irrationality of faith.

Galeazzo Mondella, known as Moderno, *The Scourging of Christ*. Silver, partially gilded. 5½ x 4 inches (14 x 10 cm). Kunsthistorisches, Vienna.

Luca Signorelli,
The Philosopher. Fresco,
Cappella di San Brizio,
Cathedral, Orvieto.

The "modern" interpretation of the Last Judgment—Luca Signorelli (1440/50–1523)

Among the array of artists privileged to work on the Sistine Chapel in Rome, the painter Luca Signorelli had already made a name for himself. Like Perugino, Ghirlandaio, and Botticelli, he belonged to the generation of artists born between 1440 and 1450 who were to dominate the art of the second half of the century. On April 5, 1499, Signorelli signed a contract with the band of cathedral architects of Orvieto, committing himself to complete the ceiling frescoes in the Brizius Chapel begun by Fra Angelico in 1447—moreover, he agreed to finish them in the style of his predecessor. In addition, in the contract Signorelli "pledges himself and promises that he will personally paint all the figures on the forenamed ceiling, in particular the faces and all parts of the figures from the midpoint upwards, and that nothing will be painted on them in Luca's absence.... And it is agreed that the said Master Luca is bound to mix all the colors himself." The contract bespeaks a practicality that attempts to exclude anything that might hinder the work from attaining its greatest potential.

Apparently Signorelli performed his task to the full satisfaction of those who commissioned him, for as soon as he was finished with the ceiling, he was given the contract for the decoration of the entire chapel. Whether or not a complete thematic program had been agreed upon with the masters of the cathedral, the self-willed Signorelli introduced a wealth of breathtaking details—from the appearance of the Antichrist, to the End of the World, to the souls' entry into Heaven or Hell—which lent the necessary weight to his visions of the fate of mankind.

Thus, at the threshold of the 16th century Signorelli created a cycle drawn from the Bible and the *Legenda aurea*, interwoven with portraits of ancient authors

Luca Signorelli,
The End of the World
(detail), 1499–1505.
Fresco. Cappella di San
Brizio, Cathedral,
Orvieto.

and illustrations from Dante's *Divine Comedy*. In other words, he created a clearly developed iconography that could be understood without extraordinary scholarly knowledge. In so doing, Signorelli was fully in the trend of his times. With the completion of his work, the tradition of the programmatic painting of a room reaches a highpoint that is only superseded by the frescoes completed by Michelangelo in the Sistine Chapel. Signorelli's masterpiece, with its "heathenish" nakedness, grotesque figures, and portraits of ancient philosophers, would no longer have been possible even a few decades later.

As Signorelli was starting his work, the most recent manifestation of the Antichrist from the view of the pope was the reformer monk Savonarola, who had just been burned in Florence. As a result, bugaboo scenarios of the end of the world were livelier than usual, as often occurs at the turn of a Christian century.

In the spirit of the times, Signorelli's first fresco depicts the evil deeds of the Antichrist that directly prefigure the end of the world: Fiery rain, a flood, and an earthquake destroy all, causing soldiers, women, and children seemingly to leap in panic out of the painting into the chapel. There, David and the Sibyl of Cumae sit with the book of wisdom and watch as their prophecies come true.

Signorelli takes the resurrection of the flesh literally. Skeletons as well as already "reincarnated" souls creep out of the earth, which is soft enough to allow them to push their way through, but hard enough to support a person's weight. Full of expectation, the figures are grouped as on an empty stage. Signorelli's work is a unique compendium of

Ever since the 14th century, Dante's journey through the *Inferno*, *Purgatorio*, and *Paradiso* has been edited, interpreted, and illustrated more frequently and in more varied ways than any other work. Just between 1477 and 1502, editions of the *Divine Comedy* appeared in Foligno, Mantua, Venice, Naples, and Milan—not to mention an elaborate edition with a commentary by Cristoforo Landino (1481), illustrated in part by Botticelli, and that of Pietro Bembo (Venice, 1502).

Luca Signorelli, *The Resurrection of the Flesh*, 1499–1505. Fresco, 234 x 273 inches (600 x 700 cm). Cappella di San Brizio, Cathedral, Orvieto.

Luca Signorelli, *The Damned* (detail), 1499–1505, Fresco. Cappella di San Brizio, Cathedral, Orvieto.

nudes that portray every posture and attitude possible to the human body and skeleton, and that deeply impressed no less an artist than Michelangelo. But exactly this strongly developed plastic musculature would have probably spurred Leonardo to epithets such as a "sack of nuts" and "bundle of radishes."

Signorelli never depicted the Last Judgment; Christ as Judge is present only as a figure in the ceiling fresco. Immediately after the *End of the World*, humankind is already divided into the *Chosen* and the *Damned*, who either worship or are tormented by demons. On the left altar wall, the good ascend into heaven; on the right, the ferryman Charon rows the damned to the Underworld where Minos assigns them punishment. The basis for these events forms a high socle with scenes from *The Divine Comedy* and portraits of ancient philosophers (including Dante), all of which is embedded in a fabulous world of grotesques.

Before falling into disfavor with the Church, the painting of grotesques was a very popular style of ornamentation during the High Renaissance. Not only Signorelli, but in particular also Raphael, contributed much to their popularity by using them in the loggia of the Vatican.

Grotesques

The figures known as grotesques received their name from the place where they were discovered—under the earth. They were found on the walls of ancient buildings that were considered to be grottoes because they hid the cultural debris of past centuries. Hybrid beings of flora and fauna, of leaves that ended in human heads, and similar fantastic shapes were eagerly adopted and varied by artists of the High Renaissance. The Counter-Reformation condemned the heathenish creations and attempted to devalue them with largely denigrating explanations:
1. Grotesques are meaningless, no more than the attempt of the artist to hide his lack of ability by means of absurdity.
2. They are images of animals observed by ancient armies in foreign lands.
3. They are figures derived from Egyptian hieroglyphics.
4. They are illustrations of costumed servants at summer feasts.
5. They represent fantastic creatures from fables.
6. They illustrate the wanderings of Pythagoras's soul through various states of being.
7. Grotesques were created deliberately with no meaning to give people with nothing better to do a chance to think up absurd interpretations.

Michelangelo Buonarroti (1475–1564)

A full generation younger than his brilliant rival, Leonardo da Vinci, Michelangelo spent a short time as an apprentice to the painter Ghirlandaio before transferring to a sculpture workshop. He never thought himself as a *uomo universale*, although he composed poetry, painted, and designed buildings. In his own eyes he remained a sculptor. In fact, aside from the ceiling in the Sistine Chapel, it is still primarily for his sculptural work that he is remembered today. Even in his paintings, Michelangelo's emphasis on the plasticity and corporeality of his figures reveals his overriding fascination with sculpture.

In Florence, Michelangelo's patrons were the Medici, at whose court he came into contact with the leading Humanists of the age. After the fall of the Medici in 1494, the artist, then 19 years old, fled by way of Bologna to Venice. On his journey, he was much impressed by the sculpture of Colleoni (see illustration p. 75), as well as by the reliefs and statues of Jacopo della Quercia for San Petronio in Bologna (see illustration p. 45).

In subsequent years, Michelangelo was repeatedly drawn to Rome, where he finally was enrolled in the service of the pope in 1505. The artist's stubbornness and egocentrism, however, made for uneasy relations with the high-handed representative of Christ on earth. Between the two there developed a tense game of attraction and rejection. For example, Michelangelo was insulted by the retraction of his commission for Julius's tomb, and left Rome in a huff; it required much patient effort by the pope before a reconciliation was effected half a year later. Michelangelo resumed work on the tomb itself, however, only after the death of the pope. Michelangelo also looked back in bitterness to the problems he faced with Julius's successors: "I feel that I lost my whole youth after being bound to this tomb monument, and I have braced myself against Pope Leo and Pope Clement as much as I could; and my all-too-great trust, that no one wanted

Michelangelo, *Pietà*, 1498–1499. Marble, height 67¾ inches (174 cm). San Pietro, Vatican, Rome.
The youthful Mary has submitted herself to her fate serenely and humbly as she gazes at her dead son, whom she holds on her knees. In this *Pietà*, one of Michelangelo's few completed sculptures, the classical beauty of the figures is loaded with a sensitivity hitherto unknown in Florentine art.

Michelangelo, *L'anima dannata* (detail). Charcoal on gray paper, 11¾ x 7¾ inches (30 x 20 cm). Galleria degli Uffizi, Florence.

Michelangelo, *The Dying Slave*, 1513. Marble, height 89⅛ inches (229 cm). Musée du Louvre, Paris.

Michelangelo, *The Creation of Adam* (detail), 1511–1512. Fresco, 109¼ x 222⅖ inches (280 x 570 cm). Sistine Chapel, Vatican, Rome.
"The more a relief resembles painting," wrote Michelangelo in 1547 to the Humanist Benedetto Varchi, "the weaker it is, and the more a painting is like a relief, the better the painting is." Michelangelo applied this maxim in an exemplary manner in his painting.

to recognize, ruined me. Such is my fate!" Pope Leo X, a Medici, had known Michelangelo from his childhood in Florence; nonetheless, this pope, too, was apparently cowed by the fury of the artist. Sebastiano del Piombo wrote in 1520 to his friend and colleague: "[The pope] told me that you grew up together, and he let me understand that he knows and loves you; but you arouse fear in anyone, even the pope."

The fruit of the reconciliation with Julius II was the commission to paint the ceiling of the Sistine Chapel, for which—according to Michelangelo—the pope gave him free reign. Thus while Raphael, who had been in Rome since 1508, was painting the chambers of the Vatican, the so-called *Stanzas*, Michelangelo embarked upon what was to be his greatest masterpiece in painting. The irritated relations between the two great masters proved to be animating. At Raphael's death, Michelangelo was still convinced that everything of value in the work of his younger colleague had been learned from him, Michelangelo.

Between 1509 and 1512, fragments of a universe were conjured into existence on the ceiling of the Sistine Chapel. The crucial events in human history (according to Michelangelo), reaching from the Creation of the world to the Great Flood, were drawn from sources in the Old Testament. Three frescoes each are devoted to the Creation, to the story of Adam and Eve, and to the story of Noah. This arch, stretching from the creation to the destruction of the world, is

Michelangelo,
*Ceiling Frescoes of the
Sistine Chapel* (detail),
1511–1512, Vatican,
Rome.

surrounded by prophets and sibyls. What statement is the artist making with this sequence, and why does he choose precisely these scenes? Could he not just as well have worked in the story of Cain and Abel, or the Tower of Babel? Of the nine pictorial fields, the three central frescoes depict the creation of humans and their relation to God; in the first three, God alone is active, and in the last three, people, when left to their own devices, follow a path to destruction. Even though Michelangelo's details follow the biblical texts very closely, his selection of scenes constitutes a novelty in biblical interpretation. Formally, the painted architecture of the ceiling, with its socles and thrones, conveys the impression that the new scenes for their part are only ceiling paintings in a tightly constructed building inhabited by prophets and sibyls.

David

Michelangelo often spent months in the marble quarries at Carrara selecting his stone, but for his *David* he turned to a piece that had lain in Florence since 1464. The band of cathedral workshops commissioned the artist to produce a monumental statue by the year 1504. On the jury that was to determine where the statue would be placed sat all the great Florentine masters (p. 126): Leonardo, Botticelli,

Michelangelo, *David*, 1501–1504. Marble, height 13 feet (400 cm). Galleria dell'Accademia, Florence.

Filippino Lippi, as well as Antonio and Giuliano da Sangallo. Politics were the determining factor in selecting the plaza in front of the portal of the Palazzo Vecchio. Just as earlier with the *David* and the *Judith* of Donatello, Michelangelo's *David* became a symbol of the freedom and watchfulness of the Florentine commonwealth. In his hovering between concentration and relaxation, *David* also embodies the Humanist ideal of the union of corporeal beauty and mental strength, as well as victory won through intelligence and skill. Michelangelo's *David* is thus the "porter" of the City Hall, dominating the entire plaza in front of the seat of government, which is dedicated to the people of Florence.

Raphael (Raffaello Sanzio, 1483–1520)

As long as the influence of his teacher Perugino was dominant in Raphael's work, the artist remained merely a second-rate Perugino. Not until he liberated himself from the clutches of his master's provincially lyric style of presentation did the young painter's unique qualities come to light. Once in Florence, Raphael was exposed to the works of Fra Bartolomeo, Leonardo, and Michelangelo, which were to have a decisive influence on his own art. In the *Marriage of the Virgin*, Raphael took the first decisive steps away from his teacher and toward a new sense of life and movement in his figures. Nonetheless, Perugino's ideal of female

Raphael, *Marriage of the Virgin*, 1504. Oil on wood, 66⅗ x 45½ inches (170 x 117 cm). Pinacoteca di Brera, Milan. The influence of Raphael's teacher, Perugino (see p. 84), is still clearly evident in this work.

beauty, which he constantly glorified in his paintings, remained with Raphael throughout his life, albeit in a modified form. "In order to paint a beautiful woman," the painter wrote in 1514 to Baldassare Castiglione, making use of ancient topos, "I must look at several beautiful women—and indeed, with you, so that we can together select the best individual features from each. But because there is a lack of art connoisseurs as well as beautiful women, I usually turn to a certain inner image."

In 1507 Raphael completed his *Carrying to the Grave*, which had been commissioned by the Baglioni family of Perugia as a memorial for their son who had been killed during civil disturbances. The painting clearly reflects the helpless pain of the victim's mother. The funeral procession has arrived at the place of burial, and the dead Christ is carried by his dearest friends to his last rest. It is, however, almost certain that the strikingly youthful bearer is a portrait of the deceased young man, who in this fashion is portrayed as doing the last honor for Christ.

Initially, on Bramante's recommendation, Raphael was supposed to paint the Vatican *Stanzas*, or state chambers of the pope, in collaboration with a number of other artists, but later the field of colleagues narrowed down to his friend Sodoma. In the end, however, the *Stanzas* came to represent the high point of Raphael's classicism. The idea for the decoration of the chambers probably stemmed from the court Humanists and Pope Julius II himself: The painter was to work up variations on older models, but at the same time the *Stanzas* as a whole were also supposed to

Fra Bartolomeo (1472–1517), *Deposition from the Cross*, 1516. Oil on wood, 61½ x 77½ inches (158 x 199 cm). Galleria Palatina, Palazzo Pitti, Florence.

With his clear, emotional style, the monk from the monastery of San Marco had as great an effect on his friend Raphael as did Michelangelo and Leonardo da Vinci.

Raphael, *Carrying to the Grave*, 1507. Oil on wood, 71¾ x 68½ inches (184 x 176 cm). Galleria Borghese, Rome.

Raphael, *The School of Athens*, 1508–1512. Fresco, width 25 feet (770 cm). *Stanza della Segnatura*, Vatican, Rome.

illustrate the theme of Church renewal. In Raphael's treatment, the first room, the *Stanza della Segnatura*, is an expression of the ideals of the High Renaissance. The four walls depict Poetry, Philosophy, Justice, and Theology as inhabiting equivalent spheres. The so-called *School of Athens* is devoted to Philosophy and the Natural Sciences, and stands across from the *Disputà* (*Disputation over the Sacrament*), a theological convocation of saints and scholars discussing the Eucharist. On the ceiling are female allegorical figures corresponding to the wall painting below, and *putti* holding tablets containing texts with the corresponding mottoes. Above the *School of Athens*, Philosophy (i.e., the recognition of causes) sits on a throne; similarly, above *Parnassus* sits Poetry (divine inspiration); above *Disputà*, Faith (knowledge of divine matters); and finally, above *Jurisprudence*, Justice (the principle of to each his own).

The *School of Athens* is in no way a historical painting, as its title and some interpretations suggest. It does not depict any actual meeting of historical figures. Beneath the monumental statues of Apollo and Minerva, the presumably most important philosophers and natural scientists have gathered, along with representatives of the liberal arts of Grammar, Arithmetic, Geometry, Astronomy, Physics, and Dialectics. The idealized architecture, reminiscent of Bramante, seems absolutely appropriate to the worthy gathering, and the entire upper half of the fresco is devoted to the arched halls of the academy. Just as Brunelleschi is given credit for the architectural representation in Masaccio's *Trinity* fresco (see p. 50), so it has been suspected that Bramante himself may have created the *Athens* architecture.

In the middle of the room, as the most important representative of the guild of philosophers, stand Aristotle and Plato (whose resemblance to Leonardo da Vinci cannot be overlooked). Plato is pointing toward heaven, as if in reference to his influence on Christian theology. In contrast, the more rational and worldly Aristotle gestures toward the earth. In front of them, Diogenes is lying on the steps. Far to the right, Zoroaster (with a celestial globe) and Ptolemy (with an earthly globe) are turning toward Raphael and his companion (possibly his friend Sodoma). The elderly bald man with a tablet in his hand is either Euclid or Archimedes (possibly with the facial features of Bramante); he appears to be illustrating the laws of proportion as they pertain to the surrounding

Ernst H. Gombrich on the *Stanzas* of Raphael

As soon as we have comprehended the general content, we are led by the rich configurations that surround us to discover new metaphors and symbolic connections.

In the process, we may sense something of that divine nimbus that for Raphael and his contemporaries surrounded all recognition. Doubtless these frescoes would have enabled many people to gain a deep insight into what at that time was known by the names of theology, poetry, and philosophy.

It is therefore not surprising that many admirers of the art of Raphael feel moved to rationalize their experience by attempting to translate the deep significance whose presence they so intensely experienced in the cycle into an equally deep philosophical statement. Raphael's greatness lay in his understanding of how to mobilize the entire tradition of pictorial composition to this end in such a way that the composition called forth just this impression of inexhaustible fullness. This inexhaustible fullness is no illusion, even if it becomes clear in the end that the instruction the artist received did not contain much more than the usual themes of contemporary school wisdom.

From: E.H. Gombrich, *Die Symbolik von Raffaels Stanza della Segnatura*, (The Symbolism of Raphael's *Stanza della Segnatura*), 1986.

architecture to the four students gathered around him. To the left we find Socrates in green robes engaged in argument, and beneath, the seated figure of the writing Pythagoras—whom Vasari took for the evangelist Matthias because of the angelic youth at his side and because of Raphael's later use of a similar figure as the apostle. All the other personages have aroused much stimulating speculation, but have never been identified with complete certainty. Heraclites has been proposed for the figure sitting on the block of stone (perhaps with the facial features of Michelangelo?); the man in the decorative armor could be Socrates's student Alcibiades, with Pericles beside him; similarly, between him and Socrates, one may find the young Xenophon.

What is important is that Julius II had the wisdom and knowledge of antiquity collected in a great hall in order for it to be displayed in his own name and in the service of the Church. It is likely that Julius housed his small private library in the *Stanza della Segnatura*, and so it is not surprising that the two central philosophers are carrying their works, the *Ethics* and *Timeos*, for Rome had by that time become the capital of the Renaissance and of Humanism—in no small part thanks to the aggressive attitude and perserverance of the reigning pope.

Raphael, *Transfiguration*, ca. 1518. Oil on wood, 160 x 109 inches (410 x 279 cm). Pinacoteca, Vatican, Rome.

Even if Raphael's early death was hastened, as Vasari relates, by his clandestine love affairs and inordinate pursuit of pleasure, an aura of divinity still surrounds the artist who both entered and

Raphael, *Sistine Chapel Madonna*, ca. 1513. Oil on canvas, 103⅓ x 76½ inches (265 x 196 cm). Gemäldegalerie, Dresden.

The peaceful pathos of the pyramidally organized composition is set against a communicative movement of the three figures. St. Sixtus, with his hand stretched out and his gaze on the Madonna, creates a direct connection between the observer and the godlike virgin; St. Barbara, a model of modesty and turned in upon herself, allows her glance to sink. The active and passive aspects of faith flank a Mother of God, stepping onto the globe of the earth, who embodies the perfection of Raphael's ideal of beauty.

Population of Italian cities during the Renaissance:

Bologna: 60,000 (1570)
Florence: 70,000 (1520)
Ferrara: 40,000 (1550)
Genoa: 60,000 (1530)
Milan: 70,000 (1550)
Mantua: 40,000 (1559)
Naples: 10,000 (1550)
Padua: 30,000 (1550)
Palermo: 70,000 (1550)
Parma: 15,000 (1517)
Perugia: 20,000 (1550)
Rome: 55,000 (1526)
Venice: 160,000 (1550)
Verona: 50,000 (1550)
Vicenza: 30,000 (1550)

departed this world on a Good Friday, and whose death was said to have been marked by an earthquake so great that it shook the Vatican buildings to their foundations. The *Transfiguration*, Raphael's last great work, also represents his own transfiguration. This glorification, however, as is so often true in such cases, has also wormed its way into Raphael's reputation. Thus, in his *Letzen Ansprache* (Last Address) from 1924, Rudolf Steiner quotes the art historian Hermann Grimm: "The only thing that one can do for Raphael personally is to write about how one picture flows into the next, as if it had been painted by a transcendental being who never really had come into contact with the earth in his mortal life."

Donato Bramante, Santa Maria della Consolazione, 1506/08–1608 (begun by Cola da Caprarola). Todi, Italy.

The enthusiam of architectural theorists for the so-called centrally planned structure was almost universal during the Renaissance. Both Alberti and Francesco di Giorgio extolled the circular form as the highest and noblest. According to Palladio, "The most beautiful and regular forms and those from which all others derive their measure are the circle and the square."

Alberti had already clearly argued the superiority of the centrally organized building over the ancient form of the basilica. Of course, Alberti recognized the secular function of the basilica in antiquity as the seat of law pronouncements as extremely honorable, for justice is, after all, a divine principle, but in the end, the basilica was not worthy enough for sacred functions.

Francesco di Giorgio also expressed enthusiasm in his architectural treatise for imaginatively designed floor plans based on the circle. Leonardo da Vinci rendered obeissance to the form with an exuberant variety of designs; Sebastiano Serlio (in his treatise on architecture after 1537) also developed a series of inspired designs for centrally planned buildings. Bramante's proposal for the rebuilding of St. Peter's, the most important church of Christendom, whose foundation was laid in 1506, lent ultimate authority to the concept.

For liturgical purposes, the central construction was inferior to a longitudinal form because it impeded communication with the congregation. Furthermore, the proper location of the altar remained a bone of contention in central construction: Should the

Antonio da Sangallo, San Biagio, 1508–1545. Montepulciano, Italy.

altar be located in the center of the church, or in the transept opposite the portal? In spite of these problems, a building based on a circle seemed most closely to approach the idea of heavenly perfection because the endless line of a circle, with no beginning and no end, symbolized eternity and mirrored the paths of the heavenly bodies. The rotundity of a building was also a Platonic image of the earth, for the ancient philosopher had deemed the earth a sphere "in which every point is equidistant from the center—the most unified and perfect of figures." For the Renaissance, the central structure possessed a self-sufficient harmony, a divine unison of the forms constituting the building.

Almost all centrally planned churches are dedicated to Mary. Vitruvius had argued that the form of a temple must correspond to the divinity for whom it was built. Mary was the Mother of God and queen of heaven—and was sometimes even depicted seated on a crescent of the moon. For her, as for the ancient goddesses Luna and Vesta, the form of a circular temple, or a central construction, was therefore most fitting.

However, critics of such convolutions of thought did not remain silent for long. Already in 1577, Carlo Borromeo, in his tract on church architecture, had begun calling for the implementation of the counter-reformatory measures of the Tridentine Council. For Borromeo, the circular form was heathenish: Only the (Latin) shape of the cross was appropriate for church architecture. His influence stretched well beyond the theory of church architecture into the actual construction of many secular buildings of the time.

The idea of central planning found its most monumental expression in the series of designs developed for St. Peter's in Rome: a massive dome placed upon a quadrant, producing a Greek cross. In actual construction, however, these plans gave way to a traditional longitudinal structure.

The debate over the value of the central structure was also reflected in painting, as demonstrated in works by Perugino, Raphael, and other masters.

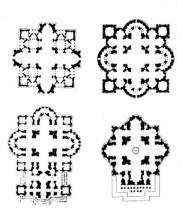

Floor plans for St. Peter's, left to right, top to bottom: Donato Bramante, 1506; Baldassare Peruzzi, ca. 1502; Antonio da Sangallo, 1539; Michelangelo Buonarroti, 1546.

Lucas van Leyden, *The Last Judgment* (center panel of a triptych), 1526–1527. Oil on wood, 84½ x 120¾ inches (217 x 310 cm). De Lakenhal Museum, Leiden.

The age of the Reformation

In the early 16th century, the Reformation movement, with its emphasis on the authority of the biblical word and its rejection of secular interference in matters of faith, held sway in the German-speaking lands north of the Alps. After the publication in 1517 of Martin Luther's 95 Theses protesting the Church's practice of selling indulgences, the movement spread quickly, but many of the Protestant princes and cities had to do battle both militarily and politically with the Catholic Emperor Charles V before finally winning official recognition of the Protestant faith in the Peace of Augsburg in 1555.

The Protestant movement was generally suspicious of pictures in houses of God—such images tempted followers in the direction of idolatry, worship of the image itself, rather than the divine which it is meant to represent. This skepticism naturally led to a reduction in commissions to artists for altar pieces, and in its extreme form, to iconoclasm. Northern art nonetheless received impulses both from cultural exchanges with Italy, whose influence was most easily conveyed through copper engravings, and from the new sense of self-confidence that developed out of increasing religious autonomy.

The elegant choreography of emotions and rich colors of the *Last Judgment* painted by Lucas van Leyden (1494?–1533) offered an exciting variation on Signorelli's treatment of the theme (see p. 120). In van Leyden's painting, the earth opens and, from the foreground to the horizon, the figures rise toward heaven. But whereas the earth has been thrown into chaos, peace has returned to heaven. Christ sits in serene majesty on the judgment seat above the apostles, who lean out from two clouds to observe and comment on what is happening. In the dramatic contrast of his composition and the delicate dynamic of the naked figures, van Leyden points toward the heights of Mannerism, which was simultaneously developing in Italy.

The Netherlandish painter Jan Gossaert (1478/88–ca. 1531), who was also known as Mabuse (after his place of birth, Maubeuge), had a firsthand acquaintance with the Italian Renaissance. After working in Antwerp from 1503 to 1507, he followed in the train of Philip of Burgundy on a tour of Italy, finally reaching Rome itself, where he undertook a series of precise drawings of scenes from ancient mythology and sculpture. Upon his return to the Netherlands Mabuse reworked his sketches into monumental paintings of the gods and mythological scenes.

Jan Gossaert, *Neptune and Amphitrite*. Oil on wood, 73⅓ x 48⅓ inches (188 x 124 cm). Gemäldegalerie, Berlin. Gossaert's naked mythological figures and images of Renaissance architecture make him one of the most important representatives of Romanism in the Netherlands.

Classical teamwork in the Netherlands: Massys and Patinir

The painters Quentin Massys (1466–1530) and Joachim Patinir (ca. 1485–1524) were both good friends of Albrecht Dürer. Like both Dürer and Gossaert, Massys was torn between northern and Italian influences. On one hand, his work reflects the traditions of Netherlandish painting and courtly elegance; on the other hand, he employed *sfumato* effects and pursued an extreme, at times consciously ugly, naturalism of the kind cultivated by such High Renaissance artists as Leonardo da Vinci. His genre-like portraits eventually had

a great influence on the Netherlandish portrayal of manners and customs. Patinir, who was according to Dürer a "landscape artist," was such a master at painting dramatic atmopheric backgrounds that the true theme of his pictures often seemed to be reduced to the peripheral.

Joachim Patinir, *The Crossing into the Underworld*, 1515–1524. Oil on wood, 25 x 40 inches (64 x 103 cm). Museo del Prado, Madrid.

Hieronymus Bosch, *Garden of Delights* (center panel of tryptich), 1505–1510. Oil on wood, 85¾ x 76 inches (220 x 195 cm). Museo del Prado, Madrid.

Pleasure and vice: Hieronymus Bosch

In both style and content, the works of Hieronymus Bosch (ca. 1450–1516) are truly eccentric and even bizarre. Born in Aachen (Aix-la-Chapelle), Bosch spent almost his entire life far from the cultural mainstream in the provincial town of Hertogenbosch, from which his name derives. The structure of his most famous work, the *Garden of Delights*, corresponds to that of a three-paneled altar painting: To the left is Paradise, and to the right Hell. But the center panel appears to have nothing to do with religion, let alone with traditional depictions of the Last Judgment with Christ as Judge and the Archangel Gabriel as enforcer.

In spite of its considerable size (the center panel measures approximately 86 x 76 inches [220 x 195 cm]; the side panels 86 x 38 inches [220 x 97 cm]), the work was apparently painted for a private customer, and possibly portrays three forms of love: heavenly, earthly, and hellish. Set in the midst of a fantastic landscape featuring utopian organic architecture, the painting seemingly presents all the forms of erotic pleasure the artist could imagine: alone, in pairs, in groups, between different races, men and women, humans and birds, strange white and black hybrid creatures, and so on. The painting achieves a harmonious balance, apparently without taking a moral standpoint, although the landscape of the *Garden* scene is much more closely related to that of the Paradise on the left than with Hell on the right.

Hieronymus Bosch, *Garden of Delights* (detail from right panel of the tryptich). Museo del Prado, Madrid.

If one considers the unusual work of Bosch in the light of the period in which he lived, his infernos of burning cities, desolate landscapes, and bizarre practices are not really so fantastic, for the immense social and economic crises that beset the Netherlands toward the end of the 15th century indeed brought violence and destruction to the land. The cities of Bruges and Ghent, which had become rich through an intelligently organized guild system particularly in the cloth industry, fell from prosperity when the English wool suppliers took up production themselves. The Netherlandish economic structure of protective tariffs, import restrictions, and warehousing rights fell apart and was forced to give way to the early capitalist model already successfully employed in the ambitious world trading harbor of Antwerp, for example. (Antwerpers, however, paid for their open-mindedness, their contacts with India and America, and the financial support of the Fuggers with an extremely unbalanced social situation, poverty, and high unemployment.)

The caricatures and grotesque mutants that populate Bosch's world are a reflection of the general religious excesses of his epoch. In particular, however, they draw from the widespread persecution of witches set in motion by Pope Innocent VIII (*Papal Bull on Witches*, 1484; *Hexenhammer*, 1491). The pope, who pursued a double set of moral standards, sought on the one hand to maintain the principles of the Church by means of witch hunts, but on the other lavishly celebrated the marriages of his illegitimate children in the Vatican. The papal laws condemned magic and sexual offenses in general, as well as deviations with devils in demonic shapes (toads and goats, etc.). The Church also specifically forbade people from metamorphizing into animals. To an even halfway enlightened individual of the age, all of this must have seemed beyond absurd—and indeed, opposition and ridicule soon arose in Humanistic circles, above all north of the Alps, where the struggle for autonomy was particularly sensitive to the exercise of church power.

In his paintings, however, Bosch surpassed all previous attempts at rendering Hell: It is not merely, for example, that individual clerics are depicted roasting in Hell, but the devils themselves are clergymen actively engaged in tormenting their charges. The scene of Hell in *The Garden of Delights* even boasts a mendicant monk in the shape of a man-eating pig (*canes domini*).

The German painter Hans Baldung, known as Grien (1484–1545), also created his own heretical world. He had learned the art of wood block printing from his friend Albrecht Dürer and, like his colleague Lucas Cranach, elaborated on the technique through the use of a second colored block. The idea of witches' magic particularly intrigued Baldung. Under the protective guise of moral outrage, he employed his wit and imagination to create an ironically sacrilegious kingdom. His *Witches' Sabbath* reveals five naked women, busily stirring up a storm in a kettle, serving a lizard instead of a lamb in a parody of the Last Supper, soaring through the air on a billy goat, and holding up a liturgical chalice out of which a toad is creeping. With their tridents, traditionally used by demons to snag wayward souls, and a cardinal's hat that will no doubt be desecrated in the course of the evening, they appear ready for all eventualities. Ominously, their only company is the devil in the form of a goat, a fat toad, and Death, signified by the skull and dead tree.

In northern climes, unlike in Italy, the nude had nothing to do with the expression of ancient ideals, but rather was associated with shame, pity, and sin.

Hans Baldung, known as Grien, *Witches' Sabbath*, 1510. *Chiaroscuro* woodcut, 14¾ x 10¼ inches (37.9 x 26 cm). British Museum, London.

Whereas the martyr Sebastian, whose athletic naked-ness provided artists with an opportunity to demon-strate their talents in the depiction of human anatomy, had advanced to the second most popular saint in Italy (after John the Baptist), in Germany the nude occured in depictions of Adam and Eve as sinners, or with the sufferings of Christ during the Passion. Not until the appearance of Luther, who accepted the pleasurable side of sexuality and even officially sanctioned its exercise for motives other than reproduction, did artists sympathetic with his views develop a more liberal approach to the naked human body. In reaction, during the Counter-Reformation, the Catholic Church strengthened its condemnation of naked and heathen representations within its sphere of influence.

Pieter Bruegel the Elder, *Hunters in the Snow* (January), 1565/66. Oil on wood, 45½ x 63¾ inches (117 x 162 cm). Kunsthistorisches Museum, Vienna.

Pieter Bruegel the Elder (1525/30–1569)

Attendants in the train of Philip II, who was on tour 1549–1550 in the northern provinces of the empire for his father, Charles V, made official note of the ugli-ness of Netherlandish women and the substantial beer con-sumption of their husbands—

but they also praised the people's cleanliness, as well as their economic and cultural accomplishments. Antwerp alone, where Bruegel had done his appren-ticeship, supported approximately 300 artists. A decade later, after Philip had succeeded to the throne in Spain and transferred the administration of the Netherlands to his half-sister Margaret of Parma, supported by the merciless Cardinal Antoine Perrenot de Granvella, tensions began to increase between the Spanish occu-pation and the Netherlanders' desire for freedom—tensions that were also expressed in art.

Unimpressed by the art of Italy (which he had visited) and the prevail-ing style of the Nether-landish Romanists, Bruegel's workshop pro-duced scenes of peas-ant life and illustrated social customs and proverbs. His work re-mained influential into the 17th century.

Bruegel's *Struggle between Carnival and Fast* portrayed this conflict symbolically. Two irreconcilable under-standings of life collide with one another in the form of

Pieter Bruegel the Elder, *Struggle between Carnival and Fast*, (detail), 1559. Oil on canvas, 46 x 64½ inches (118 x 165 cm). Kunsthistorisches Museum, Vienna.

Winter and Spring. The singing, carousing adherents of the corpulent Carnival figure, enthroned on a barrel on runners and brandishing sausage and meat on a spit, march against the train of the exhausted Lenten season, who wields only a crust of bread and two herrings as weapons. There is no hint here of any battle between good and evil, since both parties are portrayed as equally grotesque. This caricature of a painting of manners—of small town life lived out between market, church, and two inns—carries a moral and political meaning behind its cheerful and fanciful surface. In the end, the painting takes a Humanist stand, for both the foggy-minded drinkers and the blindly religious masochists have long since lost the ability to judge their situation with anything approaching reason.

As the art historian Carel van Mander recorded in his *Schilderboek* ("Picture Book") of 1604, Bruegel was already celebrated as a master of the strange and droll in his own day, and he achieved equally great fame as a landscape painter: "On his travels, he very often worked directly from nature, so that when he came back from the Alps, it was said of him that he had swallowed all the mountains and cliffs in order to carry them back home and spit them out again on canvas and panels—so great was his ability here and in other regions to get close to nature."

A kingdom for human proportion:
Albrecht Dürer (1471–1528)

Albrecht Dürer the Elder (1427–1502) was of Hungarian descent and settled as a goldsmith in Nuremberg, where he quickly found acceptance by the elite artists of the city. The history of his career, as well as that of his son, represents a showcase of the great artistic names of the era. The elder Dürer advanced from apprentice to the son-in-law of Hieronymus Holper and for a time lived in a cottage belonging to Johann Pirckheimer before buying the neighboring house of the painter Michael Wolgemut (1434–1519) and becoming chairman of the local goldsmiths. At the christening of his third child, Albrecht Dürer the Younger, no less a luminary than the important printer and publisher Anton Koburger acted as godfather.

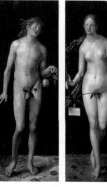

Albrecht Dürer, *Adam and Eve,* 1507. Oil on wood, each 81½ x 31¼ inches (209 x 80 cm). Museo del Prado, Madrid.

After an initial attempt at goldsmithy, the young Dürer became an apprentice to Wolgemut, but with all due humility he set his cap at being accepted for training by Martin Schongauer, who unfortunately died prematurely in 1491. Dürer had to content himself with viewing the master's work in Colmar, an event that had a decisive influence on the young artist's early style. Called back to Nuremburg by his father in 1494 to wed Agnes Frey in what should have been a good bourgeois marriage, the young man again deserted the city within a few weeks, whether in fear of the plague or the woman is left unrecorded. He

Giorgio Vasari awarded the paintings and copper engravings of Albrecht Dürer the highest praise. The artist demonstrated the "finest mastery" and produced works "so beautiful that it is impossible to surpass them in invention, organization and perspective; in buildings and costumes; in young and old heads" because, Vasari continues, Dürer always strove to replicate nature, and "to approach the Italian manner that he valued so highly." Only in the area of nude representations did Dürer's Italian admirer find fault: Dürer, according to Vasari, apparently suffered from a dearth of suitable models and had to make do in his drawings with naked apprentices, "who must have been of poor form, as is usually the case with Germans"—thus the Italian critic on the subjects of Dürer and the ugly Germans.

Albrecht Dürer, *Self-Portrait in a Fur Coat*, 1500. Oil on wood, 26 x 19 inches (67 x 49 cm). Alte Pinakothek, München.
Jakob Wimpfeling's educational tract *Über die Jugend* ("On Youth," 1500) could almost have had Dürer's self-portrait in mind as a warning: "The young man embodies such vanities and female arts of display. Nothing done by the older generation exposed them to the suspicion of the worst kind of depravity as clearly as this ridiculous and shameful hair-curling."

turns up next in the almost mythic (for German artists) city of Venice, the classical goal of the educated northern bourgeoisie—and often the source of their prosperity as well. On the wings of his Italian pilgrimage, Dürer became the first German artist to rise entirely beyond the Late Gothic and to open himself wholly to the influences of the Renaissance, in the process completing a series of self-portraits. No German artist before Dürer had attempted to come to terms with his own appearance in this manner.

Favorably situated on one of the most important European trading routes, Nuremberg had meanwhile developed into the "Venice of the North," making the most of its status as a free imperial city, local capital, and banking center second only to Augsburg. Nuremberg was governed by a small, powerful upper class of patricians who sought to nip every sign of opposition in the bud. Fearing conspiracy everywhere, they even forbade artists to organize themselves into guilds. The ire of the Church was naturally aroused by such self-determination as that shown by the Nuremberg patriarchate, who in turn eagerly accepted Luther's reforms, which offered them the double benefits of allowing them to individualize their faith and to more fully integrate the Church into their own sphere of influence.

The prosperity of a number of cities, however, did not distract from the many political crises caused by riots extending from central to southern Germany—across Hesse to Swabia and Bavaria in the south—set in motion by the call of Hans Boeheim, the Piper of Niklashausen, for the liberation and equality of the serfs in 1476.

The young Dürer greeted the new century with a *Self-Portrait in a Fur Coat* reminiscent of a painting of Christ, thus underlining his self-confidence as a secular master. Like his father, he moved in circles that cultivated a tradition of critical thought; in Basel, for example, he became acquainted with the writings of the excommunicated papal critic and former chancellor of the University of Paris, Jean Gerson (1363–1429), and became a friend of the Nuremberg Humanist Willibald Pirckheimer (1470–1539), who had studied in Padua and Pavia. Dürer much appreciated his liberation from the confines of his home city and freely exposed himself to the intellectual and artistic movements of his epoch.

In Venice, Dürer was deeply impressed by the "naked paintings of the Guelfs," the naturalness with which the Italians handled the nude, and the works of Mantegna, Carpaccio, and the Bellinis, with whom he attempted to establish personal contact. In his writing on the proportions of the human body Dürer claims, "I have found no one who has written about the measure of the human body except one superb painter in Venice calling himself Jacobus [de' Barbari]. He showed me a man and a woman that he had done according to certain measurements; and in that moment it would have been much less important to me to see an unknown kingdom than to learn his theories."

A decade later, however, when Dürer journeyed a second time to Venice, the city that had once inspired such a strong creative impulse and enthusiasm in him, he fell prey to disillusionment. Dürer had changed, but in his eyes it seemed that it was Venice that had altered: "Among the Italians, I have many good friends who warn me not to eat and drink with their painters. Many of them are enemies of mine and copy my work in the churches and wherever they can find it." He continued, "that which pleased me so much eleven years ago, does not please me anymore."

Lucas Cranach (1472–1553)

Born Lucas Moller in Kronach, Bavaria, the painter who became known as Cranach was a year younger than Dürer. In the course of his long life he acquainted himself with all areas of art and applied his striking style of drawing variously to portraits, religious themes, nature studies, and erotic subjects. Far more than any of his northern contemporaries, he busied himself

Albrecht Dürer, *Melancholy*, 1514. Copperplate engraving, 9¼ x 6½ inches (23.8 x 16.8 cm), Bibliothèque Nationale, Paris. Dürer also had tremendous influence in the areas of wood block printing and copper etchings. He completed around 350 wood cuts, including an *Apocalypse* (1498), a *Great Passion* (1496–1511), and a *Lesser Passion* (1509–1511). His *Melancholy* and *Knight, Death and Devil* are the best-known of his approximately 100 copperplate etchings.

Lucas Cranach the Elder, *Melancholy*, 1532. Oil on wood, 29½ x 21¾ inches (76 x 56 cm). Musée d'Unterlinden, Colmar.

Lucas Cranach, *The Fountain of Youth* (detail), 1546. Oil on wood, 47½ x 73 inches (122 x 187 cm). Gemäldegalerie, Berlin.

with works full of mythological references—a genre that enjoyed great favor as court art.

Cranach's *Fountain of Youth* displays one of these cheerful courtly themes: the miraculous reversal of the aging process. In carts and wagons, the old women are carried from the rocky region on the left to a pool where their youth is restored; on the right, directed by a courtier, they disappear into a tent. Men, in contrast, have no need of such a restorative bath, as their activity with the young women stationed discreetly in the bushes as well as a tablet in the foreground makes abundantly clear. Toward the front of the pool, two elderly women are discussing whether they should really undergo the procedure and whether there is any advantage in beginning the whole cycle once again.

Cranach's financial independence, his good relations with the ruling classes, and his openness to the world guaranteed him customers who appreciated his works. Close contact with Catholic leaders such as Cardinal Albrecht of Brandenburg and even Emperor Charles V did not prevent him, however, from standing witness to the marriage of his friend Martin Luther while he was court painter to the Prince Elector Frederick the Wise in Wittenberg. Cranach achieved an extremely independent position; he supported an entire group of apprentices at his own expense in his large artistic workshop, which soon rose above all North German competition. Initially his workshop engaged in something close to mass production of altarpieces for even the most remote regions; later, when the Reformation put an end to the demand, he concentrated on moralizing works from mythology and the Bible. From his friendship with Luther, the talented painter/businessman developed his firm into the leading supplier of pictures for the reformers.

In fact, the relation between Protestantism and religious art was double-edged. Idolatry, or the veneration of images rather than the persons they represent, was also rejected by the Catholic Church, but the boundaries between the two approaches were unclear and the Catholic cult of relics smelled of fetish-worship to the Protestants, who accepted pictures only as decoration. Cranach acknowledged the Reformation, putting his art at its service with his portraits of Luther, illustrations of biblical texts, pictures of the Passion, and paintings on the theme of law and grace.

Matthias Grünewald (Matthis Nithart, ca. 1480–1531/32)

Though few details of his life are known, Matthias Grünewald without doubt created the most impressive Renaissance altar north of the Alps. His painting for the chapel of the Antonite hospital in Isenheim portrays the sufferings of Christ drastically for the ailing residents. The exterior panels depicting Christ—whose body appears to be marred by leprosy and whose fingers are splayed in pain—open up to reveal Christ's divine origin in the interior. To the left is the annunciation and Christ's

Matthias Grünewald, *Crucifixion, Good Friday panel,* Isenheimer Altar, 1512–1516. Oil on wood, 105 x 119¾ inches (269 x 307 cm). Musée d'Unterlinden, Colmar.

Quentin Massys and Joachim Patinir, *The Temptation of St. Anthony*, ca. 1520. Oil on wood, 60½ x 67½ inches (155 x 173 cm). Museo del Prado, Madrid.

The team of Massys and Patinir provides a fundamentally different interpretation of this theme than Grünewald. A goblin drags the elegant monk to the ground while courtly beauties embrace him and offer an apple, which he refuses. The apple plays a role in both in the Fall from Grace and the Judgment of Paris, where the hero's choice of the goddess of love brings about destruction.

arrival from Heaven; to the right, his resurrection from the dead in a halo of light before a night sky; in the center an orchestra of angels and demons plays at his birth.

As court painter to Cardinal Albrecht of Mainz, Grünewald worked in Aschaffenburg, Seligenstadt, and Frankfurt. Unlike Dürer, he was not especially concerned with the ideals of Humanism and the stylistic achievements of the Renaissance. His use of strongly contrasting colors and *chiaroscuro*, the expressiveness of his gestures, and his ultrarealism all combine to achieve a mystic effect as well as an oppressive religious intensity.

Matthias Grünewald, *The Temptation of St. Anthony*, Isenheimer Altar. Grünewald also portrays a dance of the demons in his version of the temptation. Here, however, unlike in the Massys rendition, the devil reveals his true face.

Hans Holbein the Younger (1497/98–1543)

Of the trio of major German Renaissance artists also including Dürer and Grünewald, Hans Holbein is the youngest, and probably the most international. His career path led him from Basel to Italy, France, and the Netherlands. The increasing opposition to pictures and lack of respect for his work in his homeland drove him to travel to foreign countries. In 1524 he journeyed to Antwerp for the first time, visiting Quentin Massys and, with the recommendation of Erasmus of Rotterdam, was even able to establish himself in England, where he painted Sir Thomas More and his family and a series of portraits of King Henry VIII (and some of his wives).

Holbein's portraits found favor with the upper class and, after a futile attempt to earn respect for his artwork in his homeland and the failure of his marriage, Holbein became court painter to Henry VIII, who acted the part of an extremely cultivated regent in the first years of his reign. Through his richly naturalistic depiction of cloth, his courtly-mannerist approach, and his delicate use of symbols, Holbein made a mark for himself and developed into a leading portrait artist. The Great Plague that devastated London in 1543 also claimed the life of Holbein, and time has dealt equally unmercifully with his work, for of his monumental decorative painting on house facades in Lucerne, Basel, and London, only a few fragments remain.

Hans Holbein, *Jean de Dinteville and Georges de Selve (The Envoys)*, 1533. Tempera on wood, 80⅓ x 81½ inches (206 x 209 cm). National Gallery, London.

Holbein's paintings always keep his subject at arm's length. He portrays exteriors, avoiding deeper forays into psychology. Holbein carried the imitation of fabric and the illusionistic rendering of minute details to perfection. The strange object in the foreground of the painting is an anamorphose, or distorted image, of a skull.

1521
Conquest of Mexico under Hernando Cortéz and destruction of the Aztec kingdom
1529
Turks besiege Vienna
1532
Destruction of the high Incan culture in Peru by Francisco Pizarro
1542
Pope Paul III extends the Inquisition in Italy
1544
The Peace of Crépy ends the 4th war between Charles V and Francis I for Milan
1554
Queen Mary Tudor of England marries King Philipp II of Spain

Sacco di Roma: The end of the Renaissance?

Under the popes of the early 16th century, Rome had developed into the most glorious empire among the Italian courts, and artists willingly obeyed the summonses of the popes to participate in its glorification. The Piccolomini, the della Roveres, and the Medici families had also invited the artists to partake in what was essentially an opulent feast. But as soon as Hadrian VI stepped onto the papal throne in 1522, the glamorous unfolding of Rome's power came to an abrupt end. In addition, the leading masters of the High Renaissance had by that time disappeared: Bramante died in 1514, Bellini in 1516, Leonardo in 1519, and Raphael in 1520.

But these events were not as important as what was about to happen. In 1527, Emperor Charles V, son of Philip the Beautiful of France and Johanna the Mad of

Spain, graphically demonstrated the limits of the pope's temporal power by attacking and plundering the Eternal City. The citizens of Rome saw their defeat and humiliation as a punishment from God. They suddenly turned again to religion, sought comfort and advice from the clergy who were members of the more than 60 newly

Jakob Seisenegger, *Emperor Charles V,* 1532. Oil on canvas, 79 x 45 inches (203 x 123 cm). Kunsthistorisches Museum, Vienna.

Mannerism
Originally a disparaging term used to suggest artificiality and decadence in the Late Renaissance (1530–1600), Mannerism came to denote the exaggeration of the stylistic achievements of the Renaissance, such as the the depiction of perspective, human proportions, and naturalism to produce extremely unclear spatial alignments, ironic and playful architectural citations, contorted and elongated bodies, and strong light-dark contrasts. Mannerist techniques are most obvious in painting (in the works of Parmigianino, Bronzino, Tintoretto, and others) and in architecture (Serlio, etc.). Just as some artists of the Early Renaissance still cultivated Late Gothic tendencies, the Mannerist era also saw the persistence of certain stylistic characteristics of the High Renaissance (in Veronese, for example).

founded fraternities, and in a flurry of asceticism gave the Counter-Reformation a new impulse, which in art left its traces in the form of a renewed Catholic faith.

The new movement in the provinces

The small town of Parma lay a little distant from the blossoming cities of the Renaissance. But even here the battle cry of the Counter-Reformation did not remain unattended. With both Christian and un-Christian means, the Catholic Church stepped forward to demonstrate its right to exist, and its first step was to extend its bastions of faith. Everywhere there arose new churches and monasteries; all the religious orders subscribed to a radical renovation for themselves and their buildings—and the artists profited greatly from the new creative and financial possibilities.

Correggio, *Jupiter and Io*, 1532. Oil on canvas, 63¾ x 29 inches (163.5 x 74 cm). Kunsthistorisches Museum, Vienna.

In Parma, the two outstanding masters were Correggio (Antonio Allegri, ca. 1489–1534) and Parmigianino (Francesco Mazzola, 1503–1540). Aesthetically, both were situated between two camps. The early work of Correggio clearly reflects the influence of Mantegna and the Venetians, but later he drew more from the style of Leonardo, and finally his pictures developed— softly and sweetly—a subtle ecstasy that gave a foretaste of the dynamic of the High Baroque. Correggio became a virtuoso at altar paintings and dome frescoes, which seemed to flow effortlessly from his brush in a soft *chiaroscuro*. Mythological themes of the kind in his *Io* and *Ganymede*—both representations of being overcome with divine love—remained, however, exceptions within his *oeuvre*.

That Parmigianino also pointed to the coming Mannerist style was evident to that great defender of the pure, harmonious Renaissance ideal, Jacob Burckhardt, for whom the graceful and highly cultivated work of the Parma artist seemed "affected, yes, even repulsive." Few works aroused as much controversy as his *Madonna with the Long Neck*. Half-sitting, half-rising, the Madonna hangs in the air in an oddly formless yet elegant manner before a drawn curtain. Four children

Correggio, *Kidnapping of Ganymede*, 1532. Oil on canvas, 64 x 27½ inches (164 x 71 cm). Kunsthistorisches Museum, Vienna.

Parmigianino, *Madonna with the Long Neck*, ca. 1535. Oil on wood, 85½ x 52½ inches (219 x 135 cm). Galleria degli Uffizi, Florence.

push their way into the picture from the left, led by a boy with an amphora. In the background, a row of columns disappears with completely exaggerated line into the depths from which only a single pillar can be seen above the cloak of the Madonna. The monumentalism of the architecture is heightened by the comparatively tiny man unrolling a scroll at her feet. The ambiguity of the references combined with the somnambulant decadence and tension of the exaggerated games with perspective make the painting an excellent example of the Mannerist style.

In his epic poem *Orlando* (1516–1521), Lodovico Ariosto placed the Ferrara artists Battista and Dosso Dossi (Giovanni de Luteri, ca. 1490–1542) in the line of great master painters ranging from Mantegna and Bellini to Leonardo, Michelangelo, Raphael, Titian, and Sebastiano del Piombo. But here Vasari strongly disagreed, instead relegating the pair to ranks of the lesser masters: "The quill of Mr. Lodovico [Ariosto] brought more glory to the name of Dosso than all the brushes and paints the artist ever used during his life." And the Florentine artist-biographer did not hesitate to include a further admission that in fact probably applies to no work more appropriately than his own bible of artists: "For my part, I find that these artists were extremely fortunate to be taken up and celebrated by such great men, for the power of the pen accomplishes immeasurably much in lending credence to praise, even when the service rendered by the artist does not really measure up to it."

Vasari prevailed in this disagreement with Ariosto, and Dosso Dossi, the pupil of Lorenzo Costa, has occupied a position in art history in the second row of Late Renaissance artists. It was Dosso's fate to be inaccurately identified with his more

Parmigianino, *Self-Portrait in a Convex Mirror*, ca. 1523–24. Oil on wood, diameter 9½ inches (24.4 cm). Kunsthistorisches Museum, Vienna.

famous contemporaries. His works were often attributed to artists such as Giorgione, Titian, Paris Bordone, Raphael, or Giulio Romano—and no wonder, for in Dosso, no trace remains of the unmistakably expressive style that once distinguished the entire Ferraran School. Instead, Dosso unites the eccentric and phantasmagoric elements of his native city of Ferrara with a fine feel for color, an approach that lends all his paintings a romantic tone and works to particular advantage in his landscapes.

The fading world power on the summit of art

The conflict between Venice and the League of Cambrai in 1508, in which almost all the Western powers—pope and emperor, France and Spain—aligned themselves against the city on the lagoon, had considerably reduced Venetian might and at least temporarily robbed the city of its *Terra ferma*, that is, of its mainland holdings along the shores of the Adriatic reaching into present-day Croatia. Nonetheless, in spite of this decline, painting and architecture once more discovered an innovative power unlike anything to be found elsewhere in Italy.

In contradiction to the official understanding of the Florentines, who considered themselves capable of generating every innovation out of themselves alone, Venetian patrons embraced foreign artists who introduced new techniques and entirely new kinds of pictures. Even through the crises of the 16th century, the area around Venice remained open to the world and to immigration. Although the Venetian guild regulations strongly favored native artists, several outsiders advanced to become leading masters of their art: The Lombardi brothers, Codussi, and Sansovino came from other parts of Italy, and Cima, Giorgione, Titian, Veronese, and Palladio from the *Terra ferma*.

Dosso Dossi, *Jupiter and Mercury*, 1530. Oil on canvas, 43¼ x 58½ inches (111 x 150 cm). Kunsthistorisches Museum, Vienna. Since the 15th century, Humanist writings had been circulating under the name of "Lucian," which offered the unusual story behind this picture: Virtue wants to accuse Fortune before Jupiter, and asks several gods for support. Among these is Mercury, who cautions Virtue to be silent, for at that very moment, Jupiter is involved in designing a new type of butterfly.

Machiavelli: *The Prince*

In his most popular work, Niccolo Machiavelli (1489–1527) analyzed the absolutist ruler as well as the ways and means of achieving and retaining power. *Il Principe* is in fact a self-help manual for princes. In 1512, when the Medicis returned to Florence and removed Piero Soderini, the *Gonfalconiere* of the Republic, Machiavelli, who had been an official in the Republic, also lost all his offices. *Il Principe* was his futile attempt to ingratiate himself with the Medicis. His crystal-clear analysis leaves behind all moral considerations raised by religion and ethics about the acquisition of power. As a result, the Counter-Reformation Pope Paul IV placed *Il Principe* on the Church's Index, or list of forbidden books, in 1557. This condemnation set in motion the posthumous infamy of the author: He was equated with the Anti-Christ, and his books were burned. Two centuries later, in 1739, Frederick the Great of Prussia undertook to contradict Machiavelli in an anonymously published tract. Among princes and philosophers, however, Machiavelli also found a number of great admirers for whom the secure existence of an absolutist state was more important than individual well-being.

For Machiavelli, a ruler's origin—whether as a scion of a ruling family, a banker, or a general—is unimportant; a leader legitimizes himself solely through his will. The strategy for willing himself to power, and what he does with it, differ according to the ruler's status.

"There is less cause for the hereditary ruler to use harshness and pressure. As a result, he will be more beloved than a usurper; and if he does not make himself hated by his vices, it is understandable that his subjects will have a natural fondness for him." (Chapter 2)

"The desire for conquest is an entirely natural and widespread characteristic. The people who expend their full power to make conquests earn praise for themselves—or at least incur no blame. When they are not strong enough, but nevertheless try for conquest at any price, they commit a culpable error." (Chapter 3)

"Whoever makes himself lord of a city accustomed to freedom without destroying the city must expect in the end to be destroyed by it." (Chapter 7)

"Whoever believes that great lords have forgotten old grievances because of their present good deeds is fooling himself." (Chapter 7)

"A ruler who depends on mercenaries will never stand on a firm foundation or be secure; for mercenaries are disunited, hungry for power, without discipline or loyalty." (Chapter 12)

"The ruler ... does not have to concern himself with accusations of cruelty if he can keep his subjects united and resigned. If he sets up a few admonitory examples, he is acting more mercifully than those whose too great mildness allows disorder to arise, leading to killing and plundering." (Chapter 17)

"Never has a ruler newly come to power disarmed his subjects; rather, if he found them weaponless, he provided them with weapons. If you arm them, you will remain in power over them; those who seemed suspicious to you will put themselves at your command if you arm them, and their loyalty will remain with you." (Chapter 20)

"I am of the opinion that it is better to be too active and aggressive than too reflective. For Fortune is a woman, and to bring her around, one must push and shove her." (Chapter 23)

Machiavelli believed that the despot Cesare Borgia had put his maxims into practice most effectively. Borgia therefore prefigured the ideal ruler.

Titian (Tiziano Vecellio, 1477/ca. 1488–1576)

It is no longer possible to determine the actual year of Titian's birth; but even if he did not in fact reach the legendary age of 99 years, his long life allowed him not only to bring to fruition the important impulses he absorbed from his teacher, Bellini, and from Giorgione, but also to develop them and finally transform them to the point that they virtually turned into their opposites.

Titian, *Assumption of the Virgin*, 1516–1518. Oil on wood, 22½ x 11¾ feet (6.9 x 3.6 m). Santa Maria Gloriosa dei Frari, Venice.

Titian entered his apprenticeship at the early, but not entirely unusual, age of nine, for masters often raised apprentices as members of their family. Mantegna, for example, was ten when he entered the workshop, Sarto was seven, and Michelangelo thirteen. To many young artists, acceptance in the substitute family seemed such a matter of course that they even adopted their master's name, as with Jacopo Sansovino and Piero de Cosimo.

Probably no painter other than Titian has contin-uously earned such unreservedly high praise for his work through the vicissitudes of the history of art. From his home in Venice he established contacts with the most influential figures of his time, working for the dukes of Ferrara, Mantua, and Urbino, and becoming court painter to Emperor Charles V in 1533. Not only his extraordinary talent, but also his sound business sense and ruthless defense of his own turf, enabled him and his large workshop to remain preeminent in Venice for decades.

To his early compositions Titian brought a distinct and sophisticated sense of repose, which was also a hallmark in the work of the Bellini brothers and of

Titian, *Mary Entering the Temple*. Oil on canvas, 10⅞ x 25¼ feet (3.35 x 7.75 m). Galleria dell' Accademia, Venice.

Titian's colleague Giorgione, who died young (see p. 109); but he finally abandoned the approach in the year of his master's death. Thus the baroque dynamism of his *Assunta* (see illustration p. 153) dominates the entire Gothic construction of the Frari church in Venice.

On the canvas of his *Mary Entering the Temple,* the painter assembled an entire aristocratic society. In the midst of a fanciful Renaissance architecture, which includes a pyramid referring back to antiquity, the small and delicate Mary ascends the mighty stairway to be received into the temple like a child entering a Venetian *scuola*. The witnesses of the event comprise notable members of the Venetian Senate, as well as numerous figures from public life, which Titian worked into realistic portraits. The portrait of a woman selling eggs at the foot of the stairs is in and of itself a brilliant atmospheric genre study.

The real legacy of Titian is his *Pietà*. In this work, the traditional subtle Venetian coloration finally melts into swampy browns, and were it not for one flickering source of light, the canvas would be completely swallowed in night. The delicately illuminated architecture of Bellini (see p. 106) has turned into a disharmonious, heavy Mannerism, just as the earlier artist's meditative figures were transformed by Titian's hand into restless ghosts. Instead of painting like Bellini with a transparent, clear light, Titian injects the effects of light into a general darkness out of which bodies appear to emerge. And under the apse adorned with a pelican

Titian, *Portrait of a Man* ca. 1512. Oil on canvas, 31½ x 25¾ inches (81.2 x 66.3 cm). National Gallery, London.

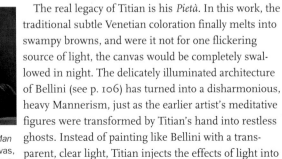

(a symbol of self-sacrifice), a strange scene is taking place. Lamenting, Mary Magdalene raises the hand of Christ and seems to be turning to a person beyond the picture on the left. Every possible trace of symmetry has been eliminated from the composition of the picture; the diagonal of the heads falls steeply from the statue of Moses, across the figures of Magdalene, Mary, and Christ, to an aged bald man in the lower right corner. There, as if the painter had forgotten a sketch of the painting at the site, leans a second small painting that repeats the entire scene, expanded by the presence of two praying men. The figure with the cross, immediately recognizable as *Fides*, the personification of faith, is armed with a script, similar to the sculpture of Moses to the left. Visibly written on the scroll is the single word "Helespontica"—perhaps an encoded reference to the desire that the Hellespont, the nub between Europe and Asia, and thus between the Christian and the Moslem world, might once again be Christianized in a kind of latter-day crusade.

This obscure final work of Titian's marks the end not only of the life of a unique artist, but also of a dramatic development in the art of Italy. The *Pietà* seems to reflect a haste and perfunctoriness in its manner of painting and a crudity in the selection of materials that seem to bespeak a weariness of the hard-won Renaissance ideals of illusion, nature, and perspective—and yet at the same time the painting represents an alternative to the usual understanding of Mannerism.

Titian, *Pietà*, 1573–1576. Oil on canvas, 12¼ x 11¼ feet (378 x 347 cm). Galleria dell' Accademia, Venice. All Renaissance achievements—corporality, natural color, illusionism—are tossed overboard by Titian in this altarpiece. Even the rustic style of the architecture, which draws the arches of the niches up to the gable, departs from the rules of Vitruvius.

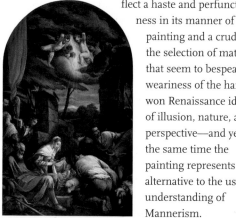

Jacopo Bassano, *Worship of the Shepherds*, 1568. Oil on canvas, 7¾ x 4⅞ feet (240 x 151 cm). San Giorgio Maggiore, Venice. Bassano, who was the founder of a dynasty of painters, also used dark brown tones in his altarpiece and preferred an artificial light source within the picture.

Tintoretto, *Ascent to the Temple*, 1552–1553. Oil on canvas, Madonna dell'Orto, Venice.

Tintoretto (Jacopo Robusti, 1518/19–1594)

Venice also produced its Mannerists. Like no other artist, Tintoretto combined fleeting and sketchy elements with drastic foreshortening, flowing corporeality, a dissolution of pictorial space, and radically vanishing perspective. As a native Venetian, he had an easier start as a painter than his great rivals Titian and Veronese. The son of a silk-dyer (Tintoretto means "little dyer"), he was inclined to the painting profession early in his life and shows a sense of color in his early work that he seemed, however, to lose with age.

According to legend, Titian immediately recognized the talent of his young pupil—and banned him from the workshop within ten days of his arrival. Whether this anecdote is true or not, it illustrates the competitive relationship between the two artists very well. At any rate, it is not possible to discover who Tintoretto's master was; it is possible that he taught himself by copying the works of Carpaccio, Titian, and other masters, even though the statutes of the guild of Venetian painters required a five-to-seven-year apprenticeship and two to three years as an associate.

In the second half of his life, Tintoretto moved into a nearly

Tintoretto, *Finding the Body of St. Mark*, 1562–66. Oil on canvas, 13 X 10¾ feet (398 x 315 cm). Galleria dell'Accademia, Venice.

monochromatic depiction of the dramatic and fleeting, which corresponds with the image of him conveyed by his biographers as an agile and extremely busy master. *The Finding of the Body of St. Mark* reveals the lightly sketched, gleaming architecture of an extremely foreshortened plaza. In the flash of lightning all the idle bystanders are caught fleeing under two arcades, while a few Christians take advantage of the confusion of the moment to steal the body of the saint from the stake in Alexandria. A camel indicates the exotic locale of the events. Among the Christians, wrapped in a noble cape, stands the patron of the picture, Tomaso Rangone, a doctor and chairman of the *Scuola Grande di San Marco*.

Paolo Veronese, *Hunter with Dog*, 1566–1568. Fresco, Villa Barbaro, Maser.
Veronese's ability to paint in an illusionistic style earned him great popularity as a fresco painter, as demonstrated here in the villa of the Humanists Marc Antonio and Daniele Barbaro, built by Palladio in 1560.

Paolo Veronese (Paolo Caliari, 1528–1588)

After his apprenticeship in Verona, Veronese arrived in Venice in 1553, where he helped Tintoretto to break up the monopoly of the old master Titian. Other than his colleagues, who devolved more and more into gloomy regions where their brown-toned paintings received meager illumination from dim light sources and fell into ever more obscure Mannerism, Veronese cultivated the cheerful, gleaming subject, which he handled with corresponding coloration. He thus directly and brilliantly led the way from the High Renaissance into the Baroque. In his *Feast in the House of Levi* (see illustration p. 158), he assembled 53 figures, two dogs, three cats, and two exotic birds around a table in an open loggia set within a clear architectural prospect. Veronese developed a splashy fantasy and coloration, combined with adventures in perspective that remained unrivaled in the 16th century, and which unmistakably reappear in the work of Tiepolo.

Veronese so successfully incorporated the experiences of his journey to Rome, and the impressions he gained viewing Michelangelo's work, with the achievements of Venetian art that he earned the motto that Tintoretto had posted over the door of his studio: "The drawing of Michelangelo and the color of Titian."

On July 18, 1573, the painter Paolo Veronese was summoned before the tribunal of the Inquisition in Venice. The minutes of that session provide not only an illuminating record of the methods and thought processes of the officials of the Holy Office, but also give us insight into the way in which an artist like Veronese understood himself and his role.

The spirit of the Counter-Reformation is to be comprehended not only in its direct persecution of the heretics north of the Alps, where the Reformation had begun, but also in the fact that the supposedly scandalous painting at issue in this case had been hanging in a monastary inoffensively for five years until it occurred to the judges that its portrayal of the Last Judgment might be objectionable.

In answering the charges, Veronese attempted to present himself as the naive, unreflecting decorative artist. He called in Michelangelo to speak as crown witness in defense of the principle of artistic freedom, and was in general willing to oblige the court with information about himself, the figures in his rendition of the Last Supper, and his handling of the biblical text:

"When asked about his profession:
Answer: I paint and draw figures.
Question: Do you understand why you have been summoned here?

A: No.
Q: Can you imagine any reasons?
A: I can well imagine them.
Q: Tell us what you think they might be.
A: I think it all has to do with what was said to me by the honorable fathers, or rather by the prior of the Monastery of Saints John and Paul, whose name I didn't know. But he explained to me that he had come here and that Your Illustrious Lordships had commanded him to have a Magdalene painted in place of a dog, and I answered him that I would gladly do all that was necessary for my honor and that of my painting, but that I did not understand how the figure of Mary

Magdalene could look good there, for many reasons which I'll relate as soon as I'm given the chance to name them.

Q: What kind of a picture were you discussing?

A: It is a painting that depicts the Last Supper that Jesus took together with his Apostles in the house of Simon.

Q: Where is this picture?

A: In the refectorium of the brothers of Saints John and Paul.

(...)

Q: Did you also paint other people into this Last Supper of Our Lord?

A: Yes.

Q: How many did you portray and what is each of them doing?

Paolo Veronese, *Feast in the House of Levi*, 1573. Oil on canvas, 18 X 41½ feet (5.55 x 12.8 m), Academy Gallery, Venice.

A: First there is the warden of the hostel, Simon, then under him a carver, whom I pictured having come for the pleasure of seeing how the matters at the table were progressing. There are many other figures there that I cannot recall, for I completed the painting quite a while ago.

(...)

Q: In the banquet scene that you painted for Saints John and Paul, what is the significance of the figure with blood streaming out of his nose?

A: He is a servant who had some kind of accident that caused a nosebleed.

Q: What is the meaning of these armed figures in German-style clothing carrying halberds?

A: At this point I must say a few words.

Q: Speak out.

A: We painters take such free-doms for ourselves, just as poets and fools do, and so I painted these halberdiers—the one drinking, the other eating at the foot of the stairs, but in any case, quite ready to do their duty, because it seemed to me both fitting and also possible that the lord of the house, who, from what I have been told, was rich and fond of splendor, must have such servants.

Q: And the one dressed as a fool with a parrot on his arm—what was your purpose in bringing him into the picture?

A: He is there as decoration, such as one usually likes to have.

Q: Who are the figures that are at the table of Our Lord?

A: The twelve Apostles.

Q: What is the first of them, St. Peter, doing?

A: He is pointing to the lamb in order to see that it is sent to the other side of the table.

Q: What is the next one doing?

A: He is holding a bowl to take what St. Peter is serving him.

Q: Tell what the third one is doing.

A: He is cleaning his teeth with a fork.

Q: Who are the persons that you really think were present at this meal?

A: I believe that only Christ and His Apostles were present; but when I have a little room left over in a painting, I decorate it with figures that I invent.

F: Did anyone order you to introduce Germans, fools, and other such figures into this painting?

A: No, but the contract allowed me to decorate it as I saw fit; the painting is large, and can contain a good many figures.

Q: Mustn't the ornamentation that a painter normally inserts into his painting have something to do with the subject and to stand in direct relationship to it, or is the matter of ornamentation left to your imagination, without choice or reason?

A: I paint after taking into consideration what is suitable and what my understanding can grasp.

Q: Does it seem fitting to you at the Last Supper of Our Lord for you to portray drunken Germans, dwarves, and other inanities?

A: Certainly not.

Q: Why did you do it then?

A: I did it under the assumption that those people were outside the place where the Last Supper took place.

Q: Don't you realize that in Germany and other places ravaged by heresy, it is the custom to degrade whatever is of concern to the holy Catholic Church and to make it appear ridiculous through images of such stupidities in order to teach false doctrine to the ignorant or unwitting populace?

A: I admit, that that is a bad thing, but I return to what I said before, namely, that for me it is a duty to follow the examples given to me by my teachers.

Q. Then what were your teachers doing? Things similar to this, perhaps?

A: In Rome, in the chapel of the pope, Michelangelo has painted Our Lord, his Mother, the saints John and Peter, and the heavenly court, and he depicted all the persons, even the Virgin Mary, for instance, naked and placed in various postures that the holiest religion never bequeathed to them.

Q: Don't you know then, that when one paints the Last Judgment, to which one is not allowed to bring any clothes, the painter has no reason to paint any? But what do these figures contain that was not inspired by the Holy Spirit? There are neither fools, nor dogs, nor weapons, nor other jokes. Does it seem to you after all of this, that you have done right to have painted your picture as you did, and do you want to demonstrate that it is good and proper?

A: No, Illustrious Lords, I have no intention to show that; but I did not think that I was doing any wrong. I hadn't taken so many things into consideration. I was far from imagining such great impropriety."

Veronese was ordered by the Inquisitorial Court to rectify the painting at his own expense.

The case of Veronese has been a matter of interest not only to art historians, but also to poets. The German poet Hans Magnus Enzensberger, for example, attempted to imagine himself in the painter's position:

"... As the sighs of the critics, the hair-splitting of the Inquisitors and the snooping of the scribes finally became too stupid for me to bear, I re-christened the Last Supper and called it Dinner at Mr. Levi's."

Abendmahl, Venezianisch, 16. Jahrhundert ("Supper, Venetian Style, 16th Century")

Palma il Vecchio (1480–1528), *La Bella,* 1525. Oil on canvas, 37 x 31¾ inches (95 x 80 cm). Museo Thyssen-Bornemisza, Madrid. In comparison with the great Venetian masters, Palma is a secondary figure. With his large figures and relative lack of originality, he is overshadowed by Titian and Lotto. The extraordinary sensuality of his glowing colors, however, had a lasting influence on the School of Bergamo.

Lorenzo Lotto, *Youth Before a White Curtain,*

1506–1508. Oil on wood, 20½ x 16¾ inches (53 x 42 cm). Kunsthistorisches Museum, Vienna.

Masters of the portrait: Lorenzo Lotto, Sebastiano del Piombo, Moretto da Brescia

In an age of individualism, it is logical that portrait painting would play a special role, and in fact many Early Renaissance artists, such as Pisanello (see p. 72), Piero della Francesca (see p. 80), and Filippino Lippi (see p. 86) helped establish the strength of this development with their own portraits. A further high point in portrait painting was reached, however, in 16th-century Venice, even though the genre of portraiture remained lower in the hierarchy of art than sacred and historical paintings—an evaluation that persists among art historians to this day.

Although Titian was one of the most highly respected portraitists of his age, his energies tended to be totally consumed with contracts from the state and from princes for impressive and weighty monumental works. With Lorenzo Lotto (ca. 1480–1556), the situation was different. Even though he completed numerous important altarpieces, he fostered portrait painting as one of his specialties, developing it with a refined naturalism interwoven with references to the character of the subject. His portrait of the serious *Youth Before a White Curtain*, with his penetrating glance, is sublime in its contrasts and handling of materials and textures. In this portrait, moreover, the painter used the opportunity to hint at the character of the sitter: The iridescently bright surface of the damask hanging behind the young man allows a glimpse into the depths behind the facade, whose darkness is dimly illuminated by a single point of light.

Contemporary biographers tended to treat Lotto with suspicion, and he could only watch helplessly when, after a promising beginning, his career seemed to be heading unremittingly toward oblivion. As a solitary painter without a workshop or pupils, he found patronage less among princes, the pope, or the emperor than in local parishes and the comparatively modest aristocracy of the provinces. Celebrated at the tender age of 25 as *Pictor celeberrimus* ("most renowned painter"), he ended his life as a poor lay brother in a monastery in Loreto. Lotto also suffered under the normative power of Tuscan judgment: Vasari mentioned this artist only in an appendix to his biography of Palma il Vecchio, where he blithely writes him off as an imitator of the Bellinis and Giorgione. It is only thanks to an exhibition of his works nearly 400 years after his death that he surfaced once more in art history.

Sebastiano del Piombo, *Portrait of a Young Roman Woman*, ca. 1512–1513. Oil on wood, 30½ x 23¾ inches (78 x 61 cm). Gemälde-galerie, Berlin.

Sebastiano del Piombo (Sebastiano Luciani, 1485–1547) left Venice for Rome in 1511, as supposedly yet another of the many victims of Titian's intrigues. In Rome, del Piombo competed against Michelangelo and his style by forging his own unique alloy of soft Venetian color design with the High Renaissance Roman repertoire of forms and dynamism. In his solution to the problem of artistic identity he thus distinguished himself clearly from his younger colleague Veronese.

The treatment of luxurious and noble materials demonstrated by Moretto da Brescia (Alessandro Bonvicino, ca. 1498–1554) in his *Portrait of a Young Man* remained unsurpassed throughout the Italian Renaissance. Golden buttons and embroidery, as well as the handle of a dagger, peep from under the wide lynx stole that sets off the subject's dark green silk coat. Before a background of marble and brocade, the young aristocrat leans on soft pink pillows in the pose of a thinker. His satin *biretta* is inscribed with Greek letters, "iou-lian-posso," a wordplay on the name of Giulio Pozzo meaning "I demand too much."

Moretto da Brescia, *Portrait of a Young Man*, 1542. Oil on canvas, 44½ x 36½ inches (114 x 94 cm). National Gallery, London.

The Florentine Mannerists

After the "classic" painters had disappeared from Florence, a vacuum existed in the city on the Arno river that could only be filled by a new generation of artists. Somewhat disillusioned, but judiciously, they stepped into the overwhelming inheritance of a Raphael, Michelangelo, and Leonardo.

Mannerism Andrea del Sarto

Andrea del Sarto,
Portrait of a Young Man,
1517–1518. Oil on
canvas, 28¾ x 22⅓
inches (72.4 x 57.2 cm).
National Gallery, London.

Andrea del Sarto (Andrea d'Agnolo, 1486–1530)

Apparently, for the artists of the Late Renaissance the favored alternative location to Florence was neither Rome nor Venice, but the court of the French kings. Remarkably, many Mannerists removed their operations to France for lengthy periods of time. Even the rather uneventful life of Andrea del Sarto reached its high point in his one-year sojourn with Francis I in 1518/19. Immediately before setting out he completed his *Madonna of the Harpies,* in which he combined a soft *chiaroscuro* with an *isfumato* effect that surrounds and softens the contrapuntal positions of the three figures in the picture.

The judgment of Vasari, who necessarily depended on hearsay, anecdotes, and interpretation for most of

Vasari's model of progress

The idea that everything continually improves, that everything constantly moves upward, has an irresistible appeal. But every step of progress inevitably reaches its endpoin . Vasari argued that antiquity presided over the greatest era of progress in the art , moving from archaic beginnings to the highest level of perfection—an opinion in which the Florentine artist was following Cicero's lead. After a period of decay in the Middle Ages, according to Vasari's *Lives of the Most Excellent Painters, Sculptors, and Architects* (1st edition, 1550), this progress repeated itself during the Renaissance. A comparison between antiquity and the Renaissance had already been drawn by Alberti (see p. 20 and 40), and even the idea of the slow upward ascent of Cimabue and Giotto was not really new, but had already become widespread in the 15th century (for example, through the Florentine Humanist Finuccini). In Vasari, the ascent of art reaches a peak in the work of Michelangelo. Leading up to this apotheosis were three phases of historical artistic development, corresponding to the three stages of life: childhood, youth, and maturity. The childhood of Renaissance art began with Giotto to Lorenzo de Bicci; its youth began with Jacopo della Quercia and ended with Signorelli. Finally, Leonardo ushered in the epoch of maturity.

Vasari's evaluative scale was based on the relation between the moment of creation of a work of art and the degree of perfection it attained. Thus a less than perfect work from 1420 can be more highly rated than an average one from 1510, for if one takes into account the "assets of the time," one would find the work of Giotto or Pisano "not beautiful, but admirable, and would take endless pleasure in seeing these first beginnings, these sparks of goodness that begin to shine forth in paintings and sculptures."

In the second phase of development, art has been "taken out of its cradle and led into its childhood." Artists cultivated their style, their drawing skills, and their powers of invention according to rules before they internalized these principles in the third phase. On the basis of their understanding, they were now able to lay aside all signs of brittle and academic dryness and move freely toward artistic perfection. Here, art managed all that "the imitation of nature allows" and rose to such heights that one must rather fear that it must once again sink, than hope that it could achieve a still higher level of perfection.

his *Lives*, knew Andrea del Sarto personally, a fact which did not make the biographer any less subjective: "Certainly it is highly regrettable when a man graced with genius, who achieves such excellence in painting, lives on the other hand such a singularly undisciplined and vice-filled life." Although del Sarto achieved neither riches nor respect during his lifetime, he was nonetheless the most important artist of the High Renaissance in Florence next to Fra Bartolomeo, and can be accounted the artistic father of the Mannerist generation.

Andrea del Sarto, *Madonna of the Harpies*, 1517. Oil on wood, 6¾ x 5¾ feet (207 x 178 cm). Galleria degli Uffizi, Florence.
The odd title refers to the small figure on the socle that was mistakenly interpreted as a harpy.

Pontormo (Jacopo Carrucci, 1494–1556) and Rosso Fiorentino (Giovanni Battista di Jacopo, 1494–1540)

These two pupils of Andrea del Sarto share not only their year of birth, but many artistic qualities as well. Both artists were already far enough removed from the epoch of the Renaissance to be aware of the significance of the art of the 15th century. They consciously quoted artists like Donatello or Uccello at a time when the principles of the rebirth of ancient ideals began to come under question. Their treatment of classical rules is marked with critical distance; furthermore, in conscious contrast to the great artists of the High Renaissance such as Leonardo, Michelangelo, and Raphael, their approach becomes nervous and demanding; they are no longer satisfied with peaceful harmony.

Rosso Fiorentino, *Deposition from the Cross*, 1527. Oil on wood, 8¾ x 6¾ feet (270 x 207 cm). San Lorenzo, Borgo San Sepolcro.

   Rosso's *Deposition from the Cross* condenses all the tensions of the new era into a single picture. The illumination of the scene ranges over a spectrum from a bright spark into almost complete darkness, just as the faces of the surging crowd range from classical beauty to monstrous distortion. In the middle, the dead Christ lies on the knees of his swooning mother,

Pontormo, *Vertumnus and Pomona*, ca. 1519–1521. Fresco, 15 X 32⅛ feet (4.6 x 9.9 m). Villa Medici di Poggio a Caiano, Florence. Whether this presentation is actually intended as a reference to the immortality of the dynasty of the Medici is a questionable, though often-proposed, theory. To interpret the naked youth as Bacchus, his female counterpart as Ceres, and the branches as a reference to the blooming family tree of the ruling Florentine family requires a great deal of sophistry—yet, it must be admitted, such inventiveness corresponds to the spirit of the age.

supported by three hands. Pain, sorrow, and horror combine into a ghostly and artificial nightmare out of which isolated effects of color flicker.

Pontormo was relatively less extreme than Rosso, particularly in his early work, and his influence was proportionally far more limited to his own region. Pontormo's figures, who often appear drenched in colored light, are characterized by their brilliant materiality, elongated bodies, and robes seemingly turned on a lath.

He did most of his work for Florentine patrons, including, of course, the Medicis. Pontormo was thus already engaged in 1519 on the family's country estate in Poggio a Caiano, which the Medici Pope Leo X and his nephew, the later Clement VII, were having furnished and decorated. There Pontormo painted the classic story of *Vertumnus and Pomona* as a fresco in a lunette. Appropriatly fitting to the villa's bucolic location, people, animals, and plants join in harmonious equilibrium in celebration of the restfulness of life in the country.

Agnolo Bronzino, *Allegory (Venus and Amor)*, ca. 1545. Oil on wood, 57 x 45¼ inches (146 x 116 cm). National Gallery, London.

Agnolo Bronzino (Angelo di Cosimo di Mariano, 1503–1572)

More so than all other portrait artists, Agnolo Bronzino, court painter to the Medici and pupil of Pontormo, produced icons of worldly decadence. Not only through the delicate skin and spiritualized faces of his protagonists, but also by means of the obvious luxury of their clothing and entire milieu, the Florentine painter put his permanent stamp on the image of Mannerism.

Cosimo de' Medici's interest in the arts and antiquity and his focus on the magnificent display of his own power did much honor to his family's name. His marriage to Eleonora of Toledo, daughter of the vice-king of Naples, offered closer contact with the Spanish court and eventually bore the newly appointed grand duke II children, as well. Both Cosimo and Eleonora were patrons of the arts, and inspired by the spirit of the court, Bronzino's career also throve under the regency of Cosimo.

Agnolo Bronzino, *Eleonora of Toledo with her Son, Giovanni de Medici,* 1550. Oil on wood, 45½ x 34¾ inches (117 x 89 cm). Galleria degli Uffizi, Florence. The duchess's love of fancy fabrics and pearls came as a welcome opportunity for Bronzino to show off his talent in reproducing textile surfaces.

Benvenuto Cellini (1500–1571) and Giambologna (Jean de Boulogne, 1529–1608)

One of the most brilliant and choleric figures of Italian art was the goldsmith and sculptor Benvenuto Cellini. Ignored and hated by many of his colleagues, he was

tolerated rather than liked by his patrons, who none-theless were intelligent enough to value his abilities. His autobiography (which no lesser a person than Goethe found so interesting that he trans-lated it immediately into German) appears to be Cellini's attempt to justify his quarrelsomeness and arrogance to future generations: Although his path is littered with the bodies of his enemies, Cellini himself always emerges the real victim.

The project which the artist carefully planned as his masterwork is *Perseus,* with which Cellini strove to prove to Florence that he was a mature sculptor

Benvenuto Cellini, *Perseus,* 1545–1554. Bronze, height 10½ feet (320 cm); with socle 16¾ feet (519 cm). Loggia dei Lanzi, Florence.

who could rightfully take his place alongside Donatello or Michelangelo. In concrete terms, *Perseus* was the thematic and technical equal of *Judith* and the stylistic counterweight to *David*, both of which were erected on the Piazza della Signoria. Whereas the unveiling of Baccio Bandinelli's group sculpture *Hercules Conquers Kakus* met with ridicule from the crowd, Cellini's *Perseus* was greeted with hymns of praise from the start—causing Bandinelli to die of jealousy, according to Cellini's account.

The monumental bronze figure of Perseus serenely offers up the decapitated head of Medusa; around the statue's base dance the four figures most important to the Perseus story: Mercury, who lent him his wings and sword; his mother Danae with the hero as a child; and the gods Minerva and Zeus. Donatello's *Judith* had already long served Florence as the Old Testament incarnation of freedom and vigilance—a service which had then been surpassed by Michelangelo's *David*. Formally and thematically, *Perseus* now completed the references to antiquity and ancient heroism.

Giambologna, *Rape of the Sabine Women*, 1579–1583. Marble, height 13½ feet (4.1 m). Loggia dei Lanzi, Florence.

Mannerist tendencies appeared in many regions of Europe in the 16th century, ranging from the works of Lucas van Leyden in the Netherlands to those of Tintoretto in Venice. In sculpture, Giambologna unites the tendencies of North and South. Born in Flanders, the artist spent most of his life at the court of the Medici in Florence, where he trained a great number of northern sculptors, including Adriaen de Vries, Pietro Francavilla, and Hans Reichle. In the second half of the century, his pupils in turn exerted a great influence on sculpture at the courts in Prague, Munich, Paris, London, and Vienna. Giambologna's own smaller bronze sculptures, because of the ease with which they could be reproduced and transported, found their way to many European cities.

On an Italian tour, which had now become virtually obligatory for any serious artist, Giambologna acquainted himself with ancient sculpture, particularly the work of Michelangelo, whom it is said he even met personally. Settling in Florence, he became court painter to Francesco de' Medici in 1561. The sculptor's convoluted composition reached a breathtaking peak with the *Rape of the Sabine Women*, an exaggerated, spiral-formed trio of figures in which the artist consciously addressed the issue of the universality of sculpture. According to Cellini's classical dictum, sculpture must present itself on at least eight sides. Giambologna went one step further by doing away with an identifiable front view, thereby requiring the viewer to take in the total impression of the piece by looking at it from all sides. Thus, like the figures themselves, the observer is also inspired to movement.

A special case: Giuseppe Arcimboldo (1527–1593)

The native Milanese Arcimboldo is first documented as an assistant to his father in the painting of the Cathedral of Milan. After laboring for a decade in the cathedral workshops of Milan, Arcimboldo sought wider horizons in 1562 at the court of Emperor Ferdinand I in Prague, where he served with bravura for 20 years as a court painter. Paolo Morigia described the nature of Arcimboldo's work in 1592: "For festivals, this noble spirit [designed] a large variety of artful, charming, and rare creations that moved all the great princes who gathered there to great amazement—and thus greatly pleased his lord and master." In other words, as Leonardo had already learned through experience, Arcimboldo's fate lay somewhere between that of an artist and a court fool. Like Leonardo, he also served the technical, engineering, and architectural needs of the emperor and his successors on the one hand, and arranged curio cabinets of the members of the imperial court on the other. This variety, along with his origin and the course of his career, make him an exceptional figure among Italian Mannerists.

left:
Giuseppe Arcimboldo, *Winter*, 1563. Oil on wood, 25¾ x 19½ inches (66 x 50 cm). Kunsthistorisches Museum, Vienna.

right:
Giuseppe Arcimboldo, *Fire*, 1563. Oil on wood, 25¾ x 19½ inches (66 x 50 cm). Kunsthistorisches Museum, Vienna. The head, composed of a collection of fruits, leaves, vegetables, books, and flames, smelts the genres of still life and portrait into an almost surrealistic composition.

Courtyard, Palace of Emperor Charles V in the Alhambra, 1527–1568, Granada, Spain.

The palaces of the French kings and of the Holy Roman Emperor—who were busily engaged in dividing Italy between them—befitted the claims of the leading contenders to world power. In the Netherlands and Spain, however, the new architectural style established itself only slowly.

In 1527, the year in which his troops sacked Rome, Charles V began work on the Alhambra in Granada. With its Renaissance design, the palace was an exception to the otherwise almost totally Gothic architecture of the Iberian Peninsula, and it constituted another jewel in the collection of the emperor, who gathered Italian art with the same pleasure and enthusiasm with which he aggrandized his empire with new territories.

In addition to the Alhambra, Philip II, Charles's successor to the throne of Spain, inherited the *Escorial,* a combination monastery and palace that was as sober as it was monumental. In such specimens of imperial architecture of domination, the sacred and profane are united in an unmistakable and absolute claim to power. Simultaneously, the pope in Rome oversaw the construction of a similarly preeminent symbol of his own power: The dome of St. Peter's Basilica. In short, the battle lines had been newly drawn.

After the political consolidation of the French royal house, the Renaissance spirit gained increasing momentum in France as a result of

Juan Bautista de Toledo/Juan de Herrera, El Escorial, 1562–1597

successful campaigns on the Italian peninsula. Out of the medieval fortress with its *donjon* arose the feudal castle, corresponding to increasing demand for comfort and culture.

The new self-confidence of a king like Charles VIII, who had gone to Italy at the age of 24 initially as a bid for peace and out of the ties of Christendom, subsequently found expression in proud and imposing architecture. Charles's successors also turned their gaze toward Italy, in matters of both politics and culture. Thus, Francis I attempted to lure artists like Raphael, Titian, and Michelangelo to his court; he was only able to successfully persuade Leonardo, Rosso Fiorentino, Cellini and a few others to work for him.

As a part of his effort to gain the imperial throne, Francis emphasized his claim with the construction of Chambord. The hunting seat, which clearly possessed the character of a monument, was formally based on the architecture of medieval French fortifications. "In the midst of intersecting halls pointing to the four corners of the earth, Francis I erected the elaborate spiraled double staircase with an open newel, overarched by a roof with a high laterne, as a symbol of royal honor richly decorated with Francis's 'F' crowned with fire salamanders and with high flaming chandeliers." (W. Prinz)

Symbolically, the axis of the world now ran in the form of the newel

Pierre Lescot, South Wing of the Louvre, (view from courtyard), begun 1546.

of a spiral staircase through the architectural monument of a king who sought to make his seat the center of earthly power.

But Chambord was not the only architectural legacy Francis I bequeathed to history: the cornerstone of the Louvre in Paris was also laid during his reign. As described by the French architectural theoretician and copperplate engraver Ducerceau in 1576, the new royal palace was "so rich in columns, friezes, archtrives, and every kind of architectural form, and is of such outstanding symmetry and beauty, that it will hardly be possible to find a second work of this sort in Europe."

Castle of Chambord, (aerial view), begun 1519.

Giulio Romano (Giulio Pippi, 1499–1546)

By the early 16th century, both the power and cultural flowering of Mantua had passed their peak under the 300-year rule of the Gonzagas (1323–1627). It was the achievement of Giulio Romano, who as a pupil of Raphael's had already participated in in the

Giulio Romano, *Fall of the Giants* (detail), 1530–1532. Fresco, Palazzo del Tè, Mantua.

painting of the *Stanzas* in the Vatican, was not only able to carry the Mantuan development one step further, but also clearly indicated the direction that late Renaissance painting and architecture would subsequently follow.

Romano'a Palazzo del Tè, the country estate house of the Gonzaga family for their day trips away from the city, distinguished itself through its painting. In place of the usual beloved gallery with its pictures of *uomini illustri,* that is, of famous figures from history, the Duke of Mantua chose to have his horse immortalized in a portrait on the wall. In the course of decorating the palazzo, the Roman painter developed a game of encoded scholarly references that he embedded in citations from ancient Roman architecture, sculpture, and painting. In the *Sala dei Giganti* the architecture itself finally seems to reel around the viewer: It appears to be falling in drastic, almost caricature-like illusion

Giulio Romano, Palazzo del Tè, view from the garden, ca. 1526–1534.

on the head of the observer, and Romano painted figures of giants who had risen up against Zeus.

Not only the virtual but also the actual architecture of the palace partially violates the usual serene harmony of the Renaissance. Asymmetry combined with details like moldings, or a sill that seems to have slipped from its proper position, made a game of traditional architectural standards.

The new power of architecture

On the whole, Mannerist tendencies remained far more restrained in architecture than in sculpture or painting. Particularly in urban buildings, however, the 16th century reached beyond the Renaissance to develop its own dramatic concepts for the entire building as well as its details.

The redesign of St. Mark's Square in Venice was undertaken by Sansovino (Jocopo Tatti, 1486–1570), who consciously counter-posed the carefully designed

Jacopo Sansovino, Biblioteca Marciana (Libreria Vecchia), 1536–1582, Venice.

plasticity of the decorative double-fronted facade of his Biblioteca Marciana against the ornamental facade of the Doge's Palace with its flat "textile" pattern. With Sansovino's design, the most imposing forum of Venice, the Piazetta and St. Mark's Square, now be-came a multi-purpose building. Behind a magnificent colonnade, he built a row of small stores and work-shops—and at the same time created a monument to literary education in a central location of the city, for the building also provided space for the library whose basic collection consisted of the donated works of Petrarch and other Latin and Greek works that had been saved from the destruction of Constantinople by the Humanist Cardinal Bessarion.

At the same time, Michelangelo was busy designing the Capitol in Rome, a trapezoidal plaza that falls away on all four sides and in the center of which would stand the ancient equestrian statue of Marcus Aurelius

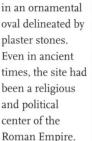

Michelangelo, Capitol, 1538–1654, Rome.

in an ornamental oval delineated by plaster stones. Even in ancient times, the site had been a religious and political center of the Roman Empire. Nine years after his sacking of the Eternal City, Charles V moved into this symbolic plaza as master of another world empire that stretched from the Netherlands to Sicily, and now even included Mexico and Peru. (Charles V had his portrait painted by Titian as the Empeor of Rome.) Charles's entry into the palace provided the impulse both for the erection of the statue of Marcus Aurelius—the incarnation of the power and dignity of Rome—at the Capitol, and for the completion of Rome's first plaza based on a single, unified design that was meant to act as a stage-like frame for viewing the city and to open onto the senatorial palace.

Among the imperial villas that of course determined the overall character of the larger surrounding area, two stand out in particular: the Villa Lante in Bafnaia and the Palazzo Farnese in Caprarola. Both were built by the theoretician and architect Giacomo Barozzi, known as Vignola (1507–1573), who worked almost exclusively for the Farnese. While Michelangelo was engaged to construct the family's city palace, which was the largest in Rome, Vignola designed a pentagonal palace as the crown of the mountain village of Caprarola. Thus, in the middle of the countryside, one of the most striking architectural monuments to a family's might and claim to power took shape. As the son of Pope Paul III, Pier Luigi Farnese (1503–47) had been given the towns of Ronciglione

Vignola, Palazzo Farnese, 1530, Caprarola.

and Nepi by his father. Pier's son Ottavio (1520–1586) married the daughter of the emperor, Margarethe of Parma, thus becoming the Duke of Parma and Piacenza at the age of 25. The ascent of the family was complete when Ottavio's son stepped into the post of vice-regent of the Netherlands in 1578.

Architecture as a status symbol and as a theatrical setting for the play of political power was a motif of the 16th century. The sacking of Rome proved to be only a temporary setback, resulting in new tasks and opportunities. The redesigning of the architecture of Rome itself and the buildings of the pope and leading families seemed to be justified also as a sign of the strength of the Catholic Church, which was arming itself for battle against the incursions of the Reformation.

Andrea Palladio (Andrea di Pietro, 1508–1580) and Venice

Born the son of a miller in Padua, the future architect became an apprentice in a stonemason's workshop in Vincenza, where he was discovered by Giangiorgio Trissino, who in all probability put the young man to work on the rebuilding of his villa in 1532. Trissino, like Alvise Cornaro before him, was a Paduan Humanist, and wanted a loggia in the High Renaissance Roman style of Bramante—a relative novelty in the vicinity of Venice. Trissino introduced the young stonemason to the writings of Vitruvius, conferred the name "Palladio" on him, and journeyed with him to Rome. There the young artist imbibed the strictures of "good" building design, the canon of ancient architecture, and that certain intellectual approach that raised architects of the day above the level of mere builders and stonemasons. The freedom and self-confidence with which Palladio juggled and varied the Roman repertoire of forms and materials became increasingly evident in the elegance and lightness of the six city palaces that he built between 1540 and 1566 in Vicenza.

When art history speaks of the Rialto Bridge in Venice, it is usually Palladio's concepts for the structure

Andrea Palladio, Palazzo Valmarana, 1565–1580, Vicenza.

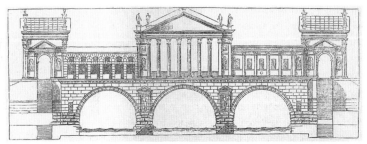

Andrea Palladio, 2nd Proposal for a Rialto Bridge. Illustration from his *Treatise*, 1570.

that are meant; the bridge that was actually built receives attention—if at all—only in relation to the architect's ideal design. The reasons why the Venetian jury, after a decade-long debate, finally decided in favor of the plans of Antonio da Ponte (ca. 1512–1597) in 1588 sheds light on the decision-making process of the government as a whole. For centuries, the Ponte di Rialto provided the only solid connection between the two main islands of Venice. Records indicate that a wooden brige, often renovated, had existed on the same site since 1172. The two surviving proposals of Palladio provide plans for either a five- or a three-arched bridge, carrying either two or four rows of small shops, as well as a central portico. The first design was clearly patterned after the antique bridges of Rome and Rimini, both of which greatly pleased and inspired the architect, and after an ancient Roman temple-shrine at the source of the Clitumnio. Next to the bridge, Palladio planned to create two large Roman-style marketplaces. Palladio's second proposal, published in an architectural treatise, is even grander. On a plateau above the water, he planned to construct a marketplace. Palladio explained that bridges are really streets over the water, and streets should be level, when possible, to make passage easier. But there can be no discussion of

Antonio da Ponte, Rialto Bridge, 1587–1591, Venice.

commodita (comfort) in Palladio's design of the Rialto, for the bridge, with its steep stairs, is in fact not at all a connection, but a hindrance to traffic. Even the market-place in his first proposal would have required a massive incursion into the old urban structure of Venice. In addition to all these problems a basic question remained: Why should a proud republic like Venice turn to Roman architecture as a communal symbol? It would be more fitting to retain what was after all a Venetian hallmark, a single-arched bridge, and to rebuild it more grandly—but such a nonclassical form was not part of Palladio's understanding of "good" architecture, as his treatise made abundantly clear. The reliable and unsurprising Antonio da Ponte, in contrast, mastered both the engineering and the artistic challenges convincingly with gently rising stairs leading over the water.

Andrea Palladio,
Il Redentore, 1577,
Venice.
Palladio built the church on the Giudecca as a pilgrims' shrine in honor of the Redeemer from the plague that swept through Venice in 1575–1577. The facade exhibits a refined intermixing and stacking of the elements of the gable, all crowned by a hemispherical dome.

Resistance to Roman, and therefore also ancient Roman, ideals had a long tradition in Venice. For this reason, the attempt to allow Palladio to rebuild the church Il Redentore on the Grand Canal as a centrally-planned building and the bid to commission Vincenzo Scamozzi (1552–1616) to rebuild Santa Maria Celeste on the model of the Pantheon failed. After the catastrophic confrontation with the League of Cambrai, the city's desire to return to its traditional culture underwent a renaissance that is particularly evident in painting. The political confusions of the subsequent years, from the war against Louis XII of France to the wars against the Turks (who, in spite of their defeat at Lepanto, wrested Cypress from Venice), engendered a desire to return to their own culture for inspiration.

Palladio, for all his virtues, lacked a feel for the finer details of a closely interwoven urban structure such as had developed over the centuries in Venice. As a result, he did not succeed in building a single palace in the city. He remained the uncompromising Humanist architect who even in Venice argued that one should place cellars and supply rooms "under the earth, where they are meant to be" (*Four Books of Architecture*,

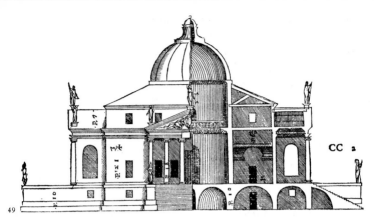

Andrea Palladio, Plan of the Villa La Rotonda, 1567, Vicenza.

chapter 2.17). This ignorance of reality goes hand-in-hand with his elitist self-understanding, whose roots reach all the way back to Alberti: Architects, they believed, should work only for the upper classes, because "their work would lose value, if it were performed for lower persons." In the same spirit, Leonardo had already stipulated that "a building should stand free on all sides in order for its true shape to be visible"—a doctrine that was virtually impossible in the dense city of Venice.

As soon as he had enough room at his disposal, Palladio developed into a unique designer of geometric spaces. This impressive rational ability established him as the leading architect of villas near Venice, where he constructed more than 20 country houses for the nobility and won enthusiastic followers among subsequent generations, particularly seen in the Palladian movement in Great Britain (led by Inigo Jones) and in many of the great public buildings of the United States.

The ideal city

Renaissance princes were entranced by the idea of immortalizing themselves not just

Andrea Palladio, Villa Barbaro. Interior view with frescoes by Veronese, 1557–1558, Maser, Treviso.

in monuments, but in a complete urban work of art—
an immense architectural project inspired by a single
concept. In such utopian thinking, utility naturally took
second place to theory. The plans tended to reflect an
absolutist attitude, expressed in austere geometical
forms. In actual practice, the application of this ideal
was problematic; the term "ideal" must be taken very
loosely if one wants to apply it to all cities laid out in a
regular pattern. And yet, ironically, both the Roman
Civita quadrata as well as modern urban blocks of
high-rise apartments are based on a clear cost-
advantage relationship, and are thus at least in the
economic sense indeed "ideal." In a
different sense, however, the term
"ideal city" implies a maximizing of
human and aesthetic qualities.

Since antiquity, people have been
imagining ideal cities (as Plato did
in *Nomoi*), but not until the Renaissance were attempts made to realize
those dreams. The utopian ideal

Bernardo Rossellino,
Palazzo Piccolomini with
the cathedral, begun in
1459, Pienza.

seems to be within reach only when a theoretical grasp
of architecture and architectural history is combined
with reflection on the social and political system at
hand. Shortly after the completion of Alberti's treatise
on architecture in 1452, Enea Silvio Piccolomini, now
Pope Pius II, initiated the first ideal city of the Renaissance when he began to design the rebuilding of his
native town of Corsignano. The palace erected on the
site of the house where he was born was decorated
with sophisticated references from his personal iconography. He designed the cathedral so that the shadow
of its facade on the equinoxes would fall precisely on
the grid of the plastered plaza. Open to the sun, it was
intended to show the course of the world and to be a
place where, at the desire of the pope, the cardinals
would come and build their own appropriate palaces.
Even when the idealistic construction remained only
fragmentary, its compactness and conception made it
unique in Renaissance architecture, and indicative of

179

Vincenzo Scamozzi, La Palmanova, 1593.

the direction taken in following centuries.

In 1564 Cosimo de' Medici had commissioned his architect, Bernardo Buontalenti (1536–1608), to build a city with the beautiful name of *Terra del sole*. Unfortunately, the project never progressed beyond the planning stage.

The construction in 1593 of *Palmanova*, the military city on the border of the Venetian territory, constituted the most complete formal actualization of the ideas of Francesco di Giorgio, Leonardo, and Filarete. This military base is not, however, an ideal city in the true sense, for there is nothing of the social organism about it; the organizing force behind the city was the unlimited power of the military, which had its own absolute priorities. The Renaissance dream of a geometrically laid out city plan appealed to many a provincial despot seeking to redesign his urban domain. Nonetheless, in Palladio's formulation, the goal always remained to have "no place that is not easily accessible to the military."

In 1554, however, Condottiere Vespasiano Gonzaga in fact attempted to apply Humanistic values to architecture. After exhaustive study of Vitruvius, he planned a rectangular layout of streets and buildings in the ancient pattern that would supposedly guarantee the inhabitants a satisfactory life, for Gonzaga was a ruler who, as noted by his biographer Ireno Affò, "considered the building of a city a more lasting fame than the destruction of cities with weapons."

Closing remarks

The 16th century was characterized by a comprehensive economic, social, and moral-political crisis that was, naturally, reflected in the various arts, which turned their back on classical norms and to some extent also on Humanistic and ancient ideals. Even the contemporaries of the age experienced their own epoch as a negative period torn by inner conflicts, a frightening and unstable time.

"Every one of us has contributed to the corruption of our century, " wrote Michel de Montaigne (1533–1592) in his essays. "Some committed treason, while others engaged in injustice, irreligion, tyranny, greed and cruelty, insofar as they are the stronger; the weaker contributed stupidity, vanity and laziness."

The limitless optimism of Humanist concepts, the belief in the dignity of humankind, who, made in the image of God, had been granted the ability to grow and even surpass its own limits, had already found individual critics in the 15th century. Indeed, it was seemingly impossible to imagine Humanism without the whetted blades of rhetoric and satire. Now, however, in the age of heart-wrenching faith, the Peasants' Revolt, and civil wars, humans were revealed to be animals that were distinguished from the lesser beasts only through their vanity, arrogance, and boundless greed. For example, the contemporary critic Traiano Boccalini (1556–1613) claimed, "The world is nothing but a store" in which all revolves around the accumulation of money. The reinterpretation of *Prudentia* exemplifies this alteration in values. Truth and honor were no longer valued as intelligent, but rather *Necessità*. Lies and betrayal, if they serve one's purpose, were the smarter alternative.

Along with Humanism, the rebirth of antiquity as a whole also was shaken in its foundations. In the light of this collapse, the existence of immutable values was also profoundly called into question, as Montaigne poetically described: "The world is merely an eternally rocking cradle. All things move back and forth without pause, the earth, the rocks of the Caucasus, the Egyptian pyramids. Even faithfulness is nothing but a somewhat slower swaying."

Glossary

Glossary

Allegory

Greek *allegorein* = to say in another manner. The representation of abstract expressions (such as love, faith, justice) through persons or, less commonly, through scenes or objects.

Arcade

Latin = arch. An arch set on columns or pillars.

Bronze cast

Casting in bronze was a technique known in many cultures and had been used in Europe since antiquity. The process flowered again during the Renaissance in the creation of monumental sculptures and a wealth of smaller pieces. As early as the late 14th century, Cennino Cennini described the technique as a means for making casts directly from nature, a process that he felt should be a part of the training in every art workshop. In 1568, Benvenuto Cellini offered an extensive description of the process.

When an object itself is not being used for the model to be cast (for the model is burned up during the process), a wax model is used, that is first covered with a coating of clay or plaster. Bronze is poured carefully into tiny channels in this layer of clay causing the wax to melt away and allowing all air to escape. After the mass cools, the plaster is chipped away, leaving a positive form in a raw state; the model is normally further worked on.

In order to make several casts—a method used by Antico since the end of the 15th century—molds are constructed of several parts that can be dismantled without breaking. For the sake of saving bronze and making the work easier, the casts were made around wax models containing a clay core affixed with nails to the outer clay layer; after the wax melted away, the core of clay remained. This process required less bronze since the resulting bronze figure was no longer solid, but contained a heart of clay.

Capital

Latin *capitellum* = little head. The upper portion of a column or pillar, which supports the weight of a ceiling, an arch, or an architrave.

Chiaroscuro

Italian for light-dark. The use of strong light and dark effects in painting.

Cinquecento

Italian for 500. The standard Italian expression for the 16th century.

Colonade

Latin *colonna* = column. A row of columns connected by horizontal beams.

Contraposition

Latin *contrapositus* = set in an opposite position. The ancient classical posture of the human body in sculpture, in which one leg carries the weight of the body. The other leg is placed slightly forward, and the corresponding shoulder is slightly raised. (For example, Michelangelo's *David*.)

Copperplate engraving

A method of intaglio printing in which a drawing is scratched into a plate of copper; paint or ink is then rubbed into the grooves and transferred onto paper. The process, which originated with goldsmiths, was developed around 1440, parallel to the professional production of paper and the invention of the printing press.

Diptych

A picture in two parts.

Fresco

Italian *fresco* = fresh. A method of wall painting by means of applying pigmented paints to still-wet plaster. This process allows the colors to be drawn into the layer of plaster itself, thus guaranteeing the painting a longer life. The plaster is applied to the wall in stages, and after each application, the surface is painted immediately. Each stage involves only as much area as can be completed in a day, that is, while the plaster was still wet. The application of fresh plaster onto an already dry wall causes a fine crack to appear. Fresco painting was already in use in antiquity.

Grisaille

French *gris* = gray. Painting in tones of gray, usually meant to imitate sculpture.

Guild

An association of artisans that guarded the interests of certain professional groups by controlling production and markets.

Iconography

Greek for description of a picture. Iconography decodes the contents of pictorial representation (through the interpretation of symbols and attributes, for example), establishes a connection between written sources and their illustrations, and researches pictorial typology.

Iconolatry

Greek for honoring a picture. This was controversial even

Glossary

in antiquity because of the perceived danger that worship of the divine image would supplant worship of the divinity itself.

Idolatry
Greek for worship of false gods.

Incrustation
Inset work in stone.

Legenda aurea
"The Golden Legends." A medieval collection of saints' legends, written or compiled by Jacobus de Voragine (before 1264). The *Legenda* remains the most important source on the lives of the saints.

Lucas Guild
An association of painters, similar to a trade union, existing since the 15th century under the patronage of St. Luke, who according to legend had painted the first portrait of the Mother of God.

Maestà
Italian for majesty. A type of Madonna, common in Italy in the 13th and 14th centuries, in which an enthroned Madonna is depicted holding her Child and surrounded by angels and saints.

Mannerism
See page 148.

Nimbus
Latin for halo. In painting, a glow of light (in the form of a circle, ring, or disk) surrounding the head of those persons who are supposed to be holy.

Oil painting
In oil painting, pigments are bound with oil, a technique that allows application of the paint in a manner ranging from a light glaze to a thick, palpably raised layer. In

contrast to tempera paint, oil allows for easy corrections and extremely soft transitions between colors. Oil painting was already known in antiquity; it was refined by van Eyck and his contemporaries in the Netherlands and spread widely from there.

Pilaster
Wall relief of a column with a base and a capital.

Portico
Latin name for a column-bearing porch covering the entry to a building. In Italy, however, the term *portici* also referred to covered arcades or pedestrian colonades in front of shops in the center of cities.

Predella
Socle of the altar tablet set above the mensa, or altar table. The predella was often used as a reliquary and/or decorated with sculpture or painting.

Proto-renaissance
Period before the Renaissance. After the Carolingian *renovatio*, which had produced a resurgence of ancient ideas among the educated classes for the first time, especially in literature and small sculptures, the Proto-renaissance of the 11th and 12th centuries gave a second important impulse to the revival of the ancient classical world, particularly visible in sculpture and architecture.

Quatrefoil
A standard Gothic figure of a cross contained in a larger circle and formed by four three-quarter circles that open toward each other.

Quattrocento
Italian for 400. The standard

Italian expression for the 15th century.

Renaissance
See page 9.

Romanism
A style of Northern European painting in the 16th century that reflects the influence of the Italian Renaissance.

Rustica
Also known as embossed work, rustica is masonry in the form of quadrants roughly hewn into the visible side of a wall and extending beyond it. Already used in antiquity, this style found application in the Middle Ages primarily on fortified buildings.

Sacra conversazione
A popular subject of Renaissance paintings, depicting an enthroned Madonna surrounded by saints (often from varying centuries) engaged with one another in a silent conversation. Unlike figures from the Middle Ages until into the 15th century, the group is not divided among several panels of a polyptych, but is gathered into a single architectural space. The *Pala de Santa Lucia*, painted in 1445 by Domenico Veneziano, a Venetian-born painter working in Florence, became the typus for later paintings of this kind. Antonello da Messina and Giovanni Bellini brought the *sacra conversatione* to its pinnacle.

Sarcophagus
Greek *sarcophagos* = flesh eater. A sculpted coffin made of stone (or more rarely, wood or metal) that was not buried, but placed in a tomb or set above ground.

Glossary

Schism
A split within the Church. The pope had moved from Rome to Avignon in 1309, thus placing himself within the reach of French royal power. In 1377 it seemed that the return of the papacy to Rome would restore order, but a majority of the college of cardinals subsequently gave their support to an antipope who once again established himself in Avignon. By 1409 the ongoing struggle had so exhausted some of the clergy that they elected a third pope. Not until 1417 was unity once again established, though the position of the Church remained weakened. The execution of the papal opponent, John Hus, in 1415 in Constance and the resulting riots in Bohemia contributed to the insecurity, which was addressed in the great Church Councils of the 15th century. Luther's Reformation at the beginning of the 16th century renewed the disagreements, marking both the high point of the schism and its temporary resolution. Until that point, the struggle had been largely conducted in the name of religion over the issue of Church offices and political influence; Luther, however, demanded a reassertion of basic Christian doctrinal content.

Sfumato
Italian for mellowed, vaporous. A method of painting in which soft, diffuse contours replace hard lines for the sake of an atmospheric rendering of the subject, especially landscapes.

Sibyl
Name given to ancient female oracles who, beginning in the 12th century, reappear in Christian art and are accorded the status of prophets.

Tempera painting
Painting technique common in the Netherlands until around 1440, and in Italy until 1500. Pigments dissolved in water and bound with egg, clay, or another substance were applied in layers to a surface (usually a wood panel). Because the layers did not blend, lines were usually sharply drawn and the colors were trans-parent and purer than those achieved with oil paint.

Tondo
A round picture or relief. The typos of the round relief was developed in the early Renaissance in Florence (for example, by Rossellino and della Robbia); the round picture in ca. 1450 (by Botticello, Signorelli, among others).

Triptych
A picture in three parts.

Vedute
Italian *vedere* = to see. A realistic representation of a city or country landscape. When elements of various locations are combined to create an imaginary scene, one speaks of a *capriccio*.

Woodcut
A form of relief printing in which a drawing is cut into a block of wood; the lines that are to be printed are left uncut on the surface of the block. Wood cutting developed in the 14th century, making it the oldest formal printmaking technique.

Teacher-Student Relationships in Italy

"Family tree" of Renaissance artists
Teacher-student relationships in Italy

Florence

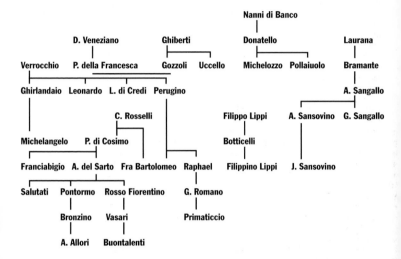

Venice

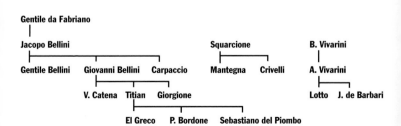

Chronology

A brief overview of the Renaissance

1363 Philip the Bold receives Burgundy as a principality

1376 The pope returns to Rome from Avignon

1385 Philip the Bold invites Sluter to the Dijon court

1401 Ghiberti wins competition for the portals of the baptistery in Florence

1408 Florence cathedral chapter commissions Donatello and di Banco to create *David* and *Isaiah*

1414 Council of Constance (until 1418)

1416 Poggio Bracciolini discovers a complete manuscript of Quintilius

1420 Construction of cathedral dome in Florence begins

1426 Masaccio works on the Brancacci chapel and paints *Trinity* fresco in Santa Maria Novella, Florence, with Masolino

1431 Council of Basel (until 1449)

1432 Van Eyck completes the Ghent Altar, Lucas Moser the Magdalen Altar, Tiefenbronn

1435 Rogier van der Weyden: *Deposition from the Cross*, Prado; Alberti: *On Painting*

1436 Paolo Uccello: Fresco of the *Equestrian Statue of John Hawkwood*, Florence cathedral; Fra Angelico begins frescoes in the monastery of San Marco, Florence

1438 Council of Ferrara

ca. 1439 Pisanello begins representations of paintings on cast medallions

1444 Federico Montefeltro becomes Duke of Urbino; Michelozzo begins the Palazzo Medici-Ricardi

1446 Fra Angelico starts painting the Nicolas Chapel, Vatican

ca. 1446 Palazzo Rucellai, Florence

1447 Pope Nicolas V founds the Vatican Library

1450 Alberti writes his treatise on architecture; Francesco Sforza becomes Duke of Milan

1451 Invention of book printing with movable type

1452 Piero della Francesca begins frescoes in San Francesco, Arezzo

1456 Donatello: Bronze *Equestrian Statue of Gattamelata*, Padua

1459 Cosimo de' Medici founds Platonic Academy in Florence

1460 Andrea Mantegna becomes court painter for the Gonzagas in Mantegna

1468 Hans Memling: *Last Judgment*

ca. 1470 Francesco del Cossa: Frescoes in The Chamber of Months, Palazzo Scifanoia, Ferrara

1471 Francesco della Rovere becomes Pope Sixtus IV, Ferrara becomes a duchy

1474 Unification of Castile and Aragon (by the marriage of Isabella I and Ferdinand V) into the Kingdom of Spain; Andrea Mantegna: *Camera degli Sposi*, Mantua

1476 Giangaleazzo Sforza is assassinated; Hugo van der Goes: *Portinari Altar*

1477 Habsburg ruler Maximilian I marries Mary of Burgundy, becoming ruler of the Netherlands

1478 Giuliano de' Medici is assassinated

1482 Sistine Chapel wall frescoes mostly complete

1483 Charles VIII becomes King of France

1484 Giambattista Cibo becomes Pope Innocent VIII; Savonarola in Florence

ca. 1485 Leonardo: *Virgin of the Rocks*, Louvre, Paris

1486 Maximilian I becomes German king

1488 Andrea del Verrocchio: *Colleoni* Statue, Venice

1489 Benedetto da Maiano: Palazzo Strozzi, Florence

ca. 1490 Giovanni Bellini: *Holy Allegory*, Florence

1492 Rodrigo Borgia becomes Pope Alexander VI

1494 Medicis expelled from Florence; Benedictine monk Savonarola rules the city; Dürer in Venice

1495 Lodovico il Moro Sforza becomes Duke of Milan; Charles VII conquers Naples

1498 Pope excommunicates Savonarola, who is burned at the stake; Louis XII crowned King of France; Michelangelo: *Pieta*, St. Peter's, Rome; Luca Signorelli begins frescoes in the Brizius Chapel in the Cathedral of Orvieto

1500 Dürer: *Self-Portrait*, Alte Pinakothek, Munich

1503 Pope Julius II

1504 Michelangelo: *Davi J*, Accademia, Florence

1505 Giorgione: *Thunderstorm*, Accademia, Venice; Giovanni Bellini: *Sacra Conversazione*, San Zaccaria, Venice; Bosch: *Garden of Delights*, Prado, Madrid

1506 New construction of St. Peter's in Rome by Bramante; discovery of an ancient Laocoon group

1508 League of Cambrai; Jacob Fugger finances the war for Emperor Maximilian I; Michelangelo: starts ceiling paintings in the Sistine Chapel, Vatican, Rome

1509 Henry VIII becomes King of England; Raphael begins *Stanzas* in the Vatican

1510 Hans Baldung Grien: *Witches Sabbath*, British Museum, London

1511 Holy League, alliance of pope, Venice, and Spain against France

1512 The Medici regain control of Florence; Mathias Grünewald: *Isenheim Altar*, Unterlinden Museum, Colmar

Chronology - Bibliography

1513 Machiavelli: *The Prince*
1514 Dürer: *Melancholy*
1515 Francis I becomes King of France
1516 Titian: *Assumption of the Virgin* in the church of Frari, Venice
1517 Martin Luther posts his 95 theses in Wittenberg; beginning of the Reformation in Germany
1519 Charles V becomes German emperor
1525 Albrecht Dürer: *Instruction for Measuring with Compass and Ruler*, first German manual for drawing proportions
1526 Palazzo del Tè in Mantua
1527 *Sacco di Roma*: Rome is plundered by troops of Charles V
1528 Baldassare Castiglione: *The Courtier*
1530 Construction of the Escorial begins; Giulio Romano: *Fall of the Giants* in Palazzo del Tè
1532 Correggio: *Io* and *Ganymede*, Kunsthistorisches Museum, Vienna
1533 Hans Holbein: *The Ambassadors*, National Gallery, London
1536 Chateau of Chambord completed; Jacopo Sansovino: Beginning of construction of the Marcus Library in Venice
1538 Michelangelo: start of work for Capitol in Rome
1545 Agnolo Bronzini: *Allegory (Venus and Amor)*, National Gallery, London
1546 Lucas Cranach: *Fountain of Youth*, Gemaldegalerie, Berlin; construction of Louvre in Paris
1550 Giorgio Vasari: *Vitae* ("Lives"; first edition)
1552 Jacopo Tintoretto: *Mary Entering the Temple*, Venice
1554 Benvenuto Cellini: *Perseus*, Florence
1559 Pieter Brueghel: *The Battle between Carnival and Fasting*
1568 Vignola: start of construction, Il Gesu in Rome
1570 Andrea Palladio: *Quattro Libri* (Treatise on Architecture)
1573 Veronese before the Inquisition
1577 Andrea Palladio: *Il Redentore*, Venice
1587 Antonio da Ponte: Rialto Bridge, Venice

Brief selected bibliography

Bora, Giulio, Maria Teresa Fiorio, Pietro C. Marani, Janice Shell, et al. *The Legacy of Leonardo: Painters in Lombardy, 1460-1530*. New York: Abbeville Press, 1998.

Elliott, Sara. *Italian Renaissance Painting*. London: Phaidon, 1993.

Fortini Brown, Patricia. *Art and Life in Renaissance Venice*. New York: H.N. Abrams, 1997.

Gombrich, E.H. *Gombrich on the Renaissance*. Vol. I: *Norm and Form*. Vol. II: *Symbolic Images*. Vol. III: *The Heritage of Apelles*. London: Phaidon, 1976.

Gombrich, E.H. *The Story of Art*, 16th ed. Englewood Cliffs, NJ: Prentice-Hall, 1995.

Hale, J.R. *The Thames and Hudson Dictionary of the Italian Renaissance*. New York: Thames and Hudson, 1995.

Hartt, Frederick. *Art: A History of Painting, Sculpture, Architecture*, 4th ed. New York: Harry N. Abrams, 1993.

Hennessy, John Pope. *Italian Gothic Sculpture*. London: Phaidon, 1996.

Hennessy, John Pope. *Italian High Renaissance and Baroque Sculpture*. London: Phaidon, 1996.

Hennessy, John Pope. *Italian Renaissance Sculpture*. London: Phaidon, 1996.

Holmes, George. *Renaissance*. New York: St. Martin's Press, 1996.

Leonardo da Vinci. *The Notebooks of Leonardo da Vinci*, ed. by Jean Paul Richter, 2 vols. New York: Dover, 1973.

Machiavelli, Niccolo, ed. by Quentin Skinner. *Machiavelli: The Prince* (1532). Cambridge Texts in the History of Political Thought. Cambridge: Cambridge University Press, 1988.

Millon, Henry A., and Vittorio Magnago Lampugnani, eds. *The Renaissance from Brunelleschi to Michelangelo: The Representation of Architecture*. New York: Rizzoli, 1997.

Palladio, Andrea. *The Four Books of Architecture*. New York: Dover, 1965.

Panofsky, Erwin. *Renaissance and Renascences in Western Art*. New York: Harper and Row, 1972.

Panofsky, Erwin. *Studies in Iconology: Humanistic Themes in the Art of the Renaissance*. Boulder, CO: Westview, 1972 (originally published in 1939).

Serlio, Sebastiano. *Tuttle l'opere d'architettura*. New Haven, CT: Yale University Press, 1996.

Turner, A. Richard. *Renaissance Florence: The Invention of a New Art*. New York: H.N. Abrams, 1997.

Vasari, Giorgio. *Lives of Italian Painters*, trans. by George Bull. Harmondsworth, UK: Penguin, 1965.

Vasari, Giorgio. *Vasari on Technique*, trans. by Louisa S. Maclehose. New York: Dover, 1960.

Index

Index

Index

Index

Photo Credits

Archiv für Kunst und Geschichte, Berlin 60, 134, 145, 146 bottom

Archivi Alinari, Florence 29, 49 bottom, 110 top, 110 bottom, 126 top, 127 bottom, 150 top, 167 bottom, 175

Artothek 15 top, 99, 142

Achim Bednorz 16, 132 top, 179

Raffaello Bencini 21, 46, 47, 49 top, 80, 81, 86 top, 88

Biblioteca Ambrosiana, Milan 18 top

British Museum, London 111 bottom, 138

Calmann & King, London (photo Ralph Liebermann) 24 left

Thorsten Droste 177

Foto Moderna, Urbino 112 bottom

Fotocelere, s.r.l. Milan 174 bottom

Germanisches Nationalmuseum, Nuremberg 101

Giancarlo Giovetti 90, 172 bottom

Lisa Hammel and Annet van der Voort 176 bottom

Kunsthistorisches Museum, Vienna (photo Lutz L. Lindner) 91, 119 bottom, 139, 140, 148, 149 top, 149 bottom, 150 bottom, 151, 162 bottom, 169 left, 169 right

Fabio Lensini 35 bottom

Paul M. R. Maeyaert 54, 70

Metropolitan Museum of Art, New York 55

Bernardino Mezzanotte 89 top

Monumenti, Musei e Galerie Ponitificie, Vatikan 95, 118, 128

James Morris 25 bottom

Museo del Prado, Madrid 58, 135, 136, 137, 141, 146 top

Museo Thyssen-Bornemisza, Madrid 162 top

National Gallery of Art, Washington 73 top, 115 bottom

National Gallery, London 56, 68, 74, 94 bottom, 108 left, 147, 154 bottom, 163 bottom, 164, 166 bottom

Nippon Television Network Corporation 124 bottom, 125

Öffentliche Kunstsammlung, Basel 64

Nicolò Orsi Battaglini 166 top

Antonio Quattrone, Studio Fotografico, Florence 42, 43, 44 left, 44 right, 48 top, 76, 77, 79, 87 bottom

Marco Rabatti und Serge Domingie 48 bottom

Rheinisches Bildarchiv, Cologne 63

Volker Rödel 132 bottom

Jean Roubier 171 top

Royal Library, Windsor 18

bottom

Scala, Florence 10, 24 right, 28, 35 top, 39 bottom, 53, 59 top, 82, 84, 93, 106, 107 top, 109 top, 111 top, 113 bottom, 123 top, 153, 155 top, 155 bottom, 165 bottom, 172 top

Toni Schneiders 100

Staatliche Graphische Sammlung, Munich 98

Staatliche Museen zu Berlin, Preußischer Kulturbesitz (photos Jörg P. Anders)
– Gemäldegalerie 25 top, 73 bottom, 89 bottom, 117, 135 top, 144, 163 top
– Kupferstichkabinett 8, 143 top

Städelsches Kunstinstitut Frankfurt (photo Ursula Edelmann) 108 right

Stadt Malmö (photo Monika Kraft) 116 top

Martin Thomas 19, 174 top

Victoria & Albert Museum, London 119 top

Walker Art Gallery, Liverpool 92 bottom

O. Zimmermann 143 bottom

Klaus Zimmermanns 22 top

Map on page 11: artic, Duisburg

The rights for all pictures not listed above lie with the author, with the publisher, or could not be ascertained.